THE PHIL SMITH COLLECTION

Happy Readings J.J....

The PHIL·SMITH COLLECTION

THOUGHTS ON LIFE, THE UNIVERSE AND ANTE-NATAL CLASSES AS HEARD ON RADIO 4

BBC BOOKS

Published by BBC Books
a division of BBC Enterprises Limited
Woodlands, 80 Wood Lane, London W12 0TT

First published 1989
© Phil Smith 1989
ISBN 0 563 20735 3

Set in 10/11 pt Times Roman by Ace Filmsetting Ltd, Frome
Printed in England by Richard Clay Ltd, Bungay, Suffolk
Cover printed by Fletchers, Norwich

CONTENTS

SMITH AND SON
    To be or not to be 8
    Nesting instincts 12
    No stomach for it 17
    Abreast of the times 21
    The twilight zone 26
    Have son, will travel 30

SMITH TAKES A BREAK
    A race apart 36
    Over Wordsworth's grave 42
    The navel of the North 48
    Foreign parts 54

SMITH INVADES THE CAPITAL
    Peg rugs and Persian carpets 62
    Termites and old school ties 66
    Parliament and pornography 71
    Odours of the abyss 75
    Live shows and dead beer 79
    I'd rather be locked in the Tower 84

SMITH ON SURVIVAL
    Bale money 90
    A lily reconsidered 94
    Those pink remembered Divis 99
    Recipe for disaster, or he who pays 103
       the pie-man mustn't call the tuna
    Wardrobe worries 107
    Keeping warm 112
    Killer instinct 116
    D-I-Y spells disaster 120
    The cost of entertainment 124

SMITH AND SON

First broadcast April 1988

TO BE OR NOT TO BE

When my wife first broke the news to me that she thought she was pregnant, my response was not one of unmitigated joy. Alas, I was on the threshold of middle age. I'd spent close on a generation attempting to avoid just such an event. I suspect it's a dilemma shared by many in the great retreat from the Pill, when couples in their thousands returned to fiddling with tinfoil packages in the dark before going to sleep with fingers crossed and a prayer on their lips. The medical and pharmaceutical professions have a lot to answer for in the fallibility of the Pill. Not the least, from men like me struggling to steady our walking-frames at the same time as leading a tot who insists on addressing us as Daddy when Grandpa would make more sense.

The dominant feeling when I first heard the news was a sense of guilt. I'd got a girl into trouble. The fact that it was my wife didn't matter. In my book, pregnancy was pronounced shame. This was the result of a simple conditioning which began in childhood. At school a girl called Lynda Baldwin had got pregnant. She was a bouncy sort of girl who wore one of those thick elastic nurse's belts round her gymslip, which had the effect of squeezing her waist in and pushing everything else out – including boys' eyes. The belt was to be her downfall. She had removed it for a car mechanic from Higson's garage, and soon she was no longer able to put it back.

The school authorities lost no opportunity of publicising the sinful nature of Jezebel Baldwin and banning elastic belts, even on boys – a move which puzzled me profoundly. The simple arithmetic of the incident was heavily underlined. Sex = sin; pregnancy = shame. For many years the sight of imminent motherhood sailing stately and ungirdled down the town's main street bearing her shame before her for all to see brought a blush of shame to my virgin cheek. And later still, when I met couples who openly admitted that they were 'trying' for a baby, I could only conclude that they were struggling to overcome their better natures and bring themselves to remove their belts.

Once this legacy of guilt was suppressed and I had rationalised away any lurking fear that my wife and I had been ruined in the eyes of decent society, more practical considerations began. An outbreak of pregnancy, like any other invasion of the system by an unexpected body, has first to be confirmed. Gone are the days when you used to have to send off to the small ads in the more dubious Sunday newspapers for a confidential service. Now it's to be had over the counter at your friendly local pharmacists. An honours degree in Chemistry, allied to nerves of tungsten, are helpful attributes in getting good results. Of the two types of pregnancy-testing kits I have sampled, both required a Doctor Jekyllian coolness in the use of pipettes, test-tubes and mirrors, at a time when a King Herod might be expected to show emotion.

Whether you plump for the brown ring or the blue dot (or a dozen colours in between, for all I know, it's such a lucrative market at between £5 and £10 every time a couple panics), it's up to you. Whatever you choose, some time will elapse before the chemical reaction takes place which will signal that all your troubles are over, or merely just a little one. Two hours to wait to know whether or not something has arrived which will stay with you for the next twenty years, or longer, if it's a cuckoo. Meanwhile my wife settled for having kittens. When the test turned out negative we threw our caps in the air and went out on a celebratory binge. I suppose it was then that we knew we didn't really want a baby.

Who could blame us? Who would choose to bring a child into a world where plutonium is becoming as common as Eurocheddar? Where the ozone belt will soon become as redundant as Lynda Baldwin's? Where Terry Wogan is on the box for six hours every night? Where Margaret Thatcher has been allowed to keep 10 Downing Street, and every town hall in the land is run from Brent?

But parenthood is nothing to do with sanity. I was born when Hitler was rampaging up and down Europe. There's no sense to procreation.

Except, what are we if we don't live on in our children? Dust blown about in dark space until there's nothing, not even a whiff of memory. What of my nose, my funny feet, my bad temper, my thirst, my utterly baffling uniqueness?

To be or not to be. The stubborn gene that came from Adam, and God knows where before that. An interplanetary speck of atoms whizzing round in the tail of a comet. A bit of the sun, and the stars, and God himself who lit the match that started the whole cosmic firework, the dance, the crawling, lurching, flying circus that tried a billion species and turned them all down until He got it right with Adam and me and Dirty Den, the Princes of Creation! How could I stop all that and throw away my bit, my precious bit that one day might make angels?

We would never have resolved all this ourselves but gone on procrastinating, if nature hadn't taken it out of our hands. The pregnancy test may have been negative but the symptoms persisted. Let down by do-it-yourself Chemistry we had to call in the professionals. Quite early one morning I appeared at the doctor's, a small bottle, still warm, in my overcoat pocket.

'Ring us tomorrow at eleven and we'll let you know.'

This is much worse than waiting thirty minutes for a blue dot. This is more like waiting for the black spot.

The patter of feet in the night. The Smiths have murdered sleep. Sleep no more! Go out no more, not without a babysitter you can trust not to burn down the house or get pregnant in front of the telly. Rest no more, so long as cars continue to hurtle down the road past the gate, and those ghastly children from the farm, who swear, come to visit.

Ignore no more the awful local schools, glue-sniffing, teenage car smashes, tight belts, unemployment, AIDS, pollution, bombs, the end of the world!

The end of the world came at eleven next morning. Over the telephone:

'Do you have the results, Doctor?'

'Yes.'

Silence. Time for a cell to divide, and divide again.

'Well?'

Now there's a head, though it looks a bit like a fish, with gills and a tail.

'What did you want the results to be?'

How am I going to answer that? To be or not to be? Dust or bits of me colonising space?

'We haven't made up our minds.'

Now there are limbs. And hands, perfectly formed fingers. And veins, like a transparent leaf pumping blood the colour of poppies.

'The result is positive.'

A lurch. The unborn child kicks inside *my* stomach. *I* feel sick. A thousand fears and uncertainties spring from the shadows.

But deep inside, far beyond reason, something has already started to glow. A sun is born. I can already feel its warmth, its light driving away the shadows.

It was the end of the world. But only one world. A comfortable world of lying in bed on Sunday mornings. An insular world where lost or battered children on TV were just news; where handicapped children were someone else's problem. A smug world where other people's kids were OK for half an hour, but after that became noisy, sticky, abominable millstones which hang-dog adults traipsed around zoos and parks while they waited for ice-lollies, had tantrums in toyshops, filled wet Sunday front-rooms with their ceaseless clamouring wants.

Yes, it was the end of a world. But was it a meaningless world? A blind corridor down which a cold wind doth blow that says at the journey's end: 'Now you are nothing. Nothing. Not even a faded picture in a grandchild's scrapbook.'

One blue spot in a test-tube and it's come to this! I'm already laid low by my parental responsibilities and it's only a tadpole. What am I going to be like when it can run towards the fire? Ride a motorbike? This is the trouble about conceiving in middle age, you can take it all too seriously. I'll bet Lynda Baldwin wasn't like this. In fact, if I remember rightly, it wasn't long before she'd squeezed herself back inside that belt and, pushing her pram, was bouncing her way round every garage in town. She's probably got teams of offspring now and wins glamorous granny competitions at Butlin's. By the time I become a granny they'll have to award it posthumously. What have I let myself in for? I reckon I've really got myself into trouble.

NESTING INSTINCTS

What does the responsible male do for the nine months that his poor spouse fills out like a spinnaker in a heavy swell? Robins fly themselves ragged, building nests. Rooks skydive under enormous twigs. Ants lug eggs as big as themselves across makeshift bridges. Each species seems to go into a frantic mode from the moment the withers cease to shake and the deed or seed is done. It's chemistry. Hormones triggering the brain, whispering, 'Hurry, hurry! You haven't long. The future is coming up the stairs, and soon you will hear the patter of soggy disposables on the lino.'

But what do I do? I already have a nest, and the larder is full of spam and dried prunes.

Half the trouble with man is that his body still thinks he's lurching about on all fours, swinging from branches and squabbling over bananas. It doesn't know yet that he's got a three-bedroomed semi, worries about hair recession, and eats TV snacks stuffed full of food additives. When he anchors on the brakes in the car because the twit in front has pulled out without signalling, the silly dumb body pumps adrenalin into his fists and shouts 'Piltdown!' to his brain.

So what do I do with this urgent energetic compulsion to gather twigs and bear daddy-long-legs to my wife? I can't sublimate it into knitting bootees or crocheting christening shawls. I thought I'd save some money by making a pram out of an old supermarket trolley, but my wife wouldn't hear of it.

There's one thing I decide I can do to compensate for the miserable male deficiency in influencing the final outcome of pregnancy. I can take charge of what my wife eats and see that only the best ingredients go into my child. My wife politely points out that she is not proposing to give birth to a Christmas cake, but it's no good. I start to treat her like a weightlifter in training for the Olympics. But the artful image-makers of today insist that a pregnant woman will only put weight on in one place. The rest must be waif-like. She must look chic and vulnerable in small floral prints and stand in sunlit rooms looking wistfully out of the window as if she wasn't quite sure where babies come from. I'm prevailed upon to reduce the portions but still insist, like a stockbreeder, that what goes in must influence what comes out. I continue to bake liver casserole for breakfast, and develop a special snack sandwich containing peanut butter, sardines, puréed spinach and yeast extract, which I call 'the master-race'.

But soon it's the elements of my wife's diet I can't control that start to obsess me. I spot a chance article in the *Daily Doom*. Extensive tests on small furry creatures with trusting brown eyes have proved that they develop malignant tumours when administered amounts of the common food additive, E320. I bound to the kitchen cupboard

and sweep out the entire contents. A sick paralysis invades my stomach, as though of paraquat I had drunk. Practically everything seems to contain the pernicious stuff. Worst of all, the potato crisps my wife has recently taken an irrational passion to, and wolfs down by the sackload, are full of it.

Now, I've no objection to a fat cat snack-food industry blackening my insides for its personal gain. I'm convinced I'm already corrupted beyond repair. But the thought of them doling out dangerous chemicals to my unborn child fills my heart with murder. I become totally paranoid overnight, and even stop jeering at organic vegetable growers and carrot juice freaks.

The modern world is an ogre bent on assailing the very quick of innocence. Our egg must be guarded like the Grail. You'd think he'd be safe, wrapped up in sleep, lapped by the soft uterine waters. But he's not. The siege of his purity begins at the very moment of conception. The filthy world reaches in to try to mar his perfection. Lead in the air, fluorine in the water, insecticides in the earth, and God knows what else in the crisps. Those aspirins she took, the gin and tonics before we knew! (The binge at Christmas!) Viruses that creep out of bottles in buildings behind barbed wire. Radiation. All that radiation. The things we don't see or hear, that we never know about.

Things that men in white coats keep to themselves, that governments button up because it's 'not in the public interest'. I put Louis MacNeice's 'Prayer Before Birth' under the mattress and murmur it every night when we turn off the lights.

> I am not yet born; oh hear me.
> Let not the bloodsucking bat or the rat or the stoat or the club-footed ghoul come near me!

I'd heard pregnancy was a pleasure. Ours has turned into a nightmare. I've seen young mothers-to-be sitting with their arms folded across their laps looking like the Mona Lisa, etherised with inner contentment. But not my wife. I've reduced her to a twitching ruin with all my worries. My latest and worst neurosis is that the damage was done long before we ever started holding hands. I have damaged genes! You see, I once went on holiday to West Cumbria. Yes, actually on holiday to within a gentle quantum hop of Sellafield, nuclear dust-bin-by-the-sea. I actually swam near where the Greenpeace people tried to block the pipeline. We had barbecues on the beach. Cooked flounders that had been nosing through the radio-active silt. A barbecue! And all the time it was me who was being barbecued. But we didn't know. No one told you in those days.

'The sea's warm today!'
'I'm tingling all over after my dip!'
'Look how the sand shines. It almost glows!'

Holy Chernobyl! What's it done to me? My chromosomes are so crippled I'm convinced I have fathered a mutant; something beyond the wildest fantasies of Steven Spielberg. Something that when it arrives to a clap of thunder will be spirited away under towels by white-faced nurses.

It's taboo to broach such things in pregnant company. At the ante-natal class bluff, fat-armed midwives specially selected for their down-to-earth approach to life turn looks of pure carbolic on such talk. Everyone may think it but no one dares ask: 'Will my child be all right?'

The midwife's solution to any ante-natal dejection is: if in doubt, start pushing. Pushing is a midwife's key to the Universe. Husbands are encouraged to attend pushing practice. It's a preparation for the supreme moment of male impotence in the delivery room. Half a dozen of us stand by, awkwardly offering feeble encouragement as the class, like a colony of basking seals, lie on their backs with their knees in the air pushing. The sight of a huge pair of yellow knickers stretched to bursting point exerts a fatal fascination over me. They are not my wife's and she's not too pleased. It's our first and last ante-natal class. We push off home, deciding to spend the rest of the nine months with our knees and fingers crossed, holding our breath. When the health worker comes round to rebuke us I tell her that natives give birth in ditches and then go straight back to work in the fields. She looks upset and writes something down in her book.

I read somewhere that pregnant mothers subjected to daily doses of oxygen produce offspring of superior brain power. (Any child of mine is going to need all the help he can get in that department.)

I whisk my wife up into the park at all hours, until one day I spot a wicked plume of yellow smoke weaving its way towards us from the chemical factory like a cobra. I rush in front of her fanning the air like a human windmill. I'm tilting at windmills all the time, I know. It's futile. Five billion people inhabit the planet and they all survived birth. Most of them are normal, give or take four million *Sun* readers.

'Pregnant wives, like growing potatoes, are best left undisturbed,' opines my dad who was fighting World War II while my mother stopped at home and pushed. That's it; maybe I should go off and wage war, build a business empire, write epic poems for Radio 3. Any of the substitute acts of creativity which we men have to solace ourselves with while women get on with the real thing. And when I've conquered, grown rich and famous, I'll come home to a tableful of small round faces who will chorus, 'Welcome home, Daddy. We missed you.'

Like heck!

NO STOMACH FOR IT

My offspring was late in arriving. I didn't blame him for wanting to stop where he was. In his boat, so would I. With his little shell ears pressed to the watery wall of the womb he'd spent nine months listening to the Nine O'Clock News and party political broadcasts. He's been jolted about by juggernauts rattling past the front-room window. He's probably also heard his father's tirades against mankind. It begins to bode well for his intelligence. Who but a born fool would want to stick his head out into such a world?

But the world, and the National Health Service, isn't going to wait.

'I think we'd better have you in,' the lady at the hospital announces to my wife, like a boating-lake attendant.

I bet more British children are born on a Friday than on any other day. By a long chalk. Why? Because to the British worker – midwives and doctors included – the weekend is sacrosanct. The humdrum business of giving birth mustn't ever be allowed to get in the way.

Come Thursday night, and young Smith still reluctant to make an appearance, it is suggested to my wife that she may like to be induced. There's not much room for refusal. All the books, all the women's features we've read, have said, 'Insist on your right to give birth to your child in the way you want. If you wish to give birth underwater, or squatting on a beanbag, insist.'

What they have failed to warn you is that the power to insist evaporates like ether the moment you step inside the corridors of the modern factory hospital. When you suddenly become a name taped to a wrist, or a chart at the foot of the bed, your resolve soon wilts under the enamelled gaze of the ward sister. And when she says, 'We're only concerned about the safety of your child,' you have to be a fanatic or a madwoman to go on insisting.

So our child is induced. Flushed out like a frightened fox. A chemical implanted into the uterus to send him scurrying to the door. 'Quite safe,' says the man in the white coat, probably thinking of his dinner party on Friday night and the need to remind his wife to chill the Chablis.

I am told to return at 9 o'clock the next morning when my wife will start to go into labour. Nine o'clock. That's nice. Office hours. How science has come to the service of mankind. It's bioculture. As predictable as harvesting a row of garden peas. One day we may have to die by the clock. 'As long as you're here before five, sir!' Not at the weekend, of course.

Despite the assurances, I spend the night curled up on the telephone table. The foreboding has come to a head. As I drive to the hospital next morning before eight, I feel like I'm making an appointment with the hangman. For someone who has always craved the extraordinary, I have never prayed so hard for normality. I want my child to be so normal he will make all civil servants look like Quentin Crisp.

Friday's peas are already being shelled when I arrive on the ward. After a delay during which I am eyed suspiciously by a group of nurses (I'm sure I hear one of them say, 'Father, did you say? Or Grandfather?') I am helped into a white smock and a hat is pushed down over my brow like a sweatband. I am a doctor now. Am I expected to do it myself? I am abandoned outside a delivery room.

I knock, with my knees. I should have had a sedative to withstand what greets me. My wife, spreadeagled on a bed full of ratchets and levers, drips and gas-masks, her feet slung high above her head in a stirrup. It's like a scene from the Chamber of Horrors. A nurse glides towards me. She's young and sweet as a flower, which instead of reassuring me makes it all seem more sinister. 'They're ready to break the waters,' she explains. An image of Barnes Wallis's bomb bounces across my brain.

An Asian doctor enters and rummages about. 'This isn't a bran-tub, this is my wife!' I want to cry. But you can't make a fuss. You are in the rubber-gloved medical machine. This is the way it is done. Your life, your dignity, your innermost innermosts in their hands.

But I wish it wasn't all so matter-of-fact, so brisk and cold, like dressing tripe. I'm not asking for much, nothing to interrupt the smooth flow of the production line. Just a nod or a wink from the doctor. Something that says, 'Hi, Dad! Things are looking good!'

Nothing to compromise the dignity of the profession. Just a nod from Olympus, Doctor. Something to acknowledge that I may have a fleeting interest in what's going on.

But our doctor came with the fixtures and fittings. With the sterile white walls, the stainless steel bowls and polished instruments, and the white lights drilling down like a Mercurian sun. Through the window only concrete blossoms in the garden. There's no relief. I'm cold and afraid for something warm and soft and vulnerable born into this hard sharp world.

I'm told that over ninety per cent of fathers are there at the birth of their children these days. I had four hours to wonder why. Four hours at the side of the bed dressed like Dr Kildare, our hands glued together by sweat, united in trying to repulse the waves of pain. Don't speak to me of magic and miracles. Childbirth is painful; visceral and bloody. Why should things we avoid, which repel us in normal circumstances, become invested with magic because they are to do with birth? I was told people make video recordings of the business. I can only marvel at the stomach some people have for things. Do they invite people for dinner, and when the holiday slides are done, serve up the birth of baby Jonathan with the petit fours?

I don't think my wife was really happy with me there – to see her at her lowest ebb, reaching down into the primal dark to drag up life.

I don't think many women are, if they're honest. Only the hysterical missionary types, those who breast-feed their children until they're five and scream for crèches in public libraries. Most women I know like to be seen by their men with their hair done and some make-up on. They'd curl up at the thought of being seen in curlers, never mind turning themselves inside out to give birth.

No, I think we men are there these days as a penance, a punishment for all those times in the past when men ignored childbirth and let her get on with it, and only appeared when it was all over to receive a washed and powdered bundle to hold in our arms and puff out our chests and think what wonderful fellows we were.

Don't mistake me. I think it's a good idea. Only don't blame us when the birth-rate falls, as it surely will. I for one won't be putting my wife through all that again.

'Come on now, Mrs Smith, push like you've been taught to.'

I told you we should have persisted with the antenatal classes. But we've never been joiners. Sitting there at the clinic with that gaggle of bell-tents discussing prams over cups of tea and ginger nuts. We missed the pushing classes. In fact, after we attended the first class and sat through a half-hour lecture on human reproduction, we decided it was all going to be a bit of a waste of time. We knew all about how it had got in. It was how we were going to get it out that concerned us.

News of when the pods are ready to pop speeds down the Friday production line. Suddenly my wife is surrounded by nurses, cabbage white butterflies fluttering in and out. My stomach knots. I am going into sympathetic contractions. Even he-men faint at this sort of thing. I just remember that I can't watch operations on televisions except through my fingers.

They've brought green cloths and spread them out ready to receive the baby. Why green, I wonder? It would make a nice change from all this white if it wasn't such a bilious colour.

My wife has been given a pain-relieving drug and drifts in and out of thirty-second sleeps which to her are separate lifetimes. Time to murder and create. I've no fingers to peep through because she has both of my hands. But something is coming out. It's so grisly. Now I know why the cloth is green. It's flecked with blood and mucus. Hands are delving in again. They've got it! It's round and purple! Is it my wife screaming, or is it me?

What is it? What have you got? Is it all right?

It's an aubergine, with testicles. A male aubergine.

He greets the white light with a wail. The first of many protests if he's really mine. The nurses turn and smile. I think they were smiles. You can't see very well through tears.

'You have a lovely little boy!'

Now it's a miracle.

ABREAST OF THE TIMES

No sooner had my son entered this strange world, gulped his first lungful of fresh air and bellowed it out again, than the army of midwives picked up their rubber gloves and abandoned us. It was Friday and the production line was at full throttle. Were they on piece work? As the doors of the delivery room slammed to, my wife and I looked at each other, dazed and uncomprehending. Suddenly we were a family. The person who had made this dramatic change in our lives had been whisked away from us and placed under a sort of incubator in the corner of the room where he was undergoing yet another change of colour. From the startling aubergine at birth his colour had subsided to a jaundiced yellow – the hue of a sick Indian who languishes in exile far away from his native sun. But apart from that, he was looking remarkably healthy. None of your wrinkled, little-old-man looks which make new parents flinch and bite their lips and wish he could be put back again until he'd filled out a bit more.

'Are you allowed to pick them up?' I enquired feebly after ten minutes had elapsed and none of the nurses had reappeared. Four hours in the hospital machine and I was hamstrung, incapable of thinking and acting for myself. Our child might well have been stamped all over with, 'Property of the NHS. Do not touch!' But something told me we should be getting to know each other, not eyeing one another from a distance like troops across no-man's-land. Were we allowed to pick him up or were his bones still setting?

It's this lack of information that's so tiresome about hospitals: a general failure to inform you about what they are doing to the bits and pieces of your own body, as if it didn't really concern you. I know that as far as the baby was concerned we should have known. We'd ploughed through everything from *Breast is Best* to *Coming of Age in Samoa*. But the birth itself is so traumatic to a beginner, so nerve-shredding, that afterwards we both sat limp as wet tissues waiting for someone to tell us we could pick up our lives again.

I not only felt chastened and humbled by what I'd seen, but I also felt superfluous, a feeble instrument in an overwhelming sense of purpose which excludes mere males. I was a sort of withered catkin that has done its bit and was waiting to drop off. My wife had every excuse for inertia. She had performed a sublime conjuring trick: a beautiful child from a lump in the bedspread. She lay back in a state of beatific fulfilment, while I stood fidgeting with my clumsy fingers like a bumpkin at the Nativity.

An absurd notion engrossed me. It was that between now and getting our baby home, someone was going to switch him. Substitute him for something inferior. We would spend the rest of our days rearing someone else's brat while our nonpareil was running around with gipsies or else being allowed to watch *Coronation Street*. Since all babies look alike to men, even their own, it was clear that I must search for some irrefutable birth-mark by which I could recognise him.

I even took out a felt-tipped pen, determined to make my own mark if I couldn't find one.

Instead of worrying about birthmarks and child-rustlers, what I should have been doing was encouraging my wife to feed him. He should have been plugged into his natural supply of milk from the outset. No one bothered to remind us to do this. And soon after being placed under the incubator our child came to the conclusion that the world he had just entered was a dreadful bore, and promptly settled down and went to sleep for forty-eight hours. That is, apart from one howling session in the middle of the night when, waking up hungry and belatedly presented with the breast, he failed to recognise its beneficial properties. After arduous attempts to interest him, a well-meaning nurse took him away and bottle-fed him, leaving us to harvest the dire consequences.

I think it was John Locke who proposed the notion that the new-born infant is a *tabula rasa*, a clean sheet upon which we adults scrawl our indelible influences. His first meal coming from a plastic bottle with a suck-fast latex teat, from that moment onwards nothing else would do. He wasn't having this breast thing that called for such a gutsy effort for such scant reward.

In a less particular age this wouldn't have mattered. My wife would have bound up her breasts and put them away for good, and we'd have happily gone ahead mixing dried milk and sterilising everything in sight until he'd learnt to chomp on sausages and mash like the rest of us.

But the 'breast is best' lobby has taken a stranglehold on middle-class motherhood. So powerful have become the paperback witchdoctors and women's mag mountebanks that any mother incapable of delivering to order as quickly and copiously as Express Dairies is made to feel inadequate, if not downright infanticidal.

We can look back on it now and see it for what it is: yet

one more piece of neo-romantic nonsense, like corn-dollies and home-baked bread; inspired by nostalgia for an imaginary golden age of innocence before science and technology deflowered mankind. Based on the myth of some buxom young peasant mother, bodice thrust aside, topping up her pink-cheeked cherub behind a hay-stook while Dad whistles happily away gathering in the harvest. Woe betide you if you don't fit the stereotype like we didn't.

We struggled day and night to try to encourage him to do it the natural way. My wife cried. I cursed. The child howled. The nursing profession was not indifferent to our plight. They sent in their equivalent of the SAS, a team of trouble-shooting midwives with centuries of service between them; shrewd and wily in the ways of wet-nursing. Bluff matrons who had supervised breech-births on top of double-decker buses, who could coax milk out of a stone with one tweak of their forceps. They did everything to persuade him to breast-feed short of unbuttoning their own ample blouses. Finally, after a night spent prowling around the house like the Macbeths while baby screamed blue murder from his chamber, it was decided to call upon the services of mechanical science. We were advised to buy a breast-pump.

Yes, I can hardly believe it myself now. The breast-pump is a truly diabolical contraption which will one day take its rightful place along with the thumbscrews and scold's bridle in a museum of torture. It's like a glass bicycle pump which sucks instead of blows. The mother clamps it on the tardy organ by means of a rubber sucker and then pumps herself for all she's worth. The milk is supposed to be drawn inside, and when it's full you stick a dummy on the end and fool baby into thinking it's the genuine man-made stuff he craves. Well, that's the theory. In practice it's impossible to operate unless the user has arms like an Irish ditch-digger. And the suction! The only fluid that appeared when we first tried was the water from my wife's eyes. Cleopatra's asp must have felt more comfortable. Eventually I ended up operating it while my wife hung on to the sucker. You can imagine the scene of domestic fulfilment as we pumped desperately away while baby howled wildly for the next few drops of supper.

Meanwhile, no-nonsense Brenda next door but two, who had her baby about the same time as ours, announced that she hadn't the slightest intention of breast-feeding her child. The idea repelled her, she admitted to a crowded supermarket check-out queue. She didn't give a disposable nappy what medical science thought. Now she's got a boy who's chewing nails while ours still has a dummy. He pulls cats' tails clean off.

The trouble with motherhood is that nobody admits they have problems. It's the female equivalent of being macho. Women will never admit to other women that life with new baby isn't as smooth as an alabaster madonna. Their very credibility as women seems to be at stake. You watch them when the prams converge on the pavement, and the only thing holding them up is the pram handle and half-a-pound of foundation on their faces, and they'll be crowing away at how well little Johnny is doing. The fact that he's bawling away every hour of the night like the wakeman and puking like a cabin boy gets forgotten in the intense rivalry as to who is the best mother and has the best baby. They're much worse than men with cars. 'Darren is crawling already. We think he tried to write his name with his rusk yesterday!' The superiority over your inert and backward specimen is implicit in every remark and gesture. 'Oh, is he still not changing his own nappy?'

My wife was dying to find someone to whom she could say, 'My God, isn't this motherhood business awful?'

As for me, I couldn't even find a father who got up in the night, let alone one who'd ever operated a breast-pump.

THE TWILIGHT ZONE

Gestation is a lovely word to describe the quiet expectation of impending motherhood – that's if you're not the mother, lumbering around on fallen arches with backache and circulation problems and all the thousand natural shocks which pregnant mums are heirs to. Yet there is no word to express the cataclysmic change which the arrival of a baby like ours signalled. For the first forty-eight hours he slept, lulled us into a false sense of calm. We had given birth to one of the fabled Seven Sleepers who would snooze away the passing of Empires. For the first time in memory our family was to welcome a calm and philosophical disposition instead of the fidgety neurotic busybodies we specialise in. We watched him sleep like a saint and smiled. We had a compliant child.

In fact, he was conserving his strength for the reign of terror to come; snatching forty winks before abandoning the practice of sleep altogether. We didn't realise it for a time, but we had produced a genetic breakthrough – a human being who would be able to stay awake through an entire Reith lecture.

You don't expect to sleep for the first few nights with a new baby. When he did sleep, I was up and down every ten minutes with a torch and feather checking that he was still breathing. I'd never realised a house was so noisy in the middle of the night. The house itself breathes.

Pipes relax with a sudden clunk, floorboards shrink and try to wriggle free of their nails, bits of mortar shutter down inside the roof-space, and something scuttles about fitfully in the loft on feet made of drawing pins. I think the whole house is slowly unbuilding itself: one of those awesome natural principles at work, something called entropy, in which the whole of creation, the cloud-capped towers, the ivory palaces, gradually disintegrate under our very noses.

These are the melancholy reflections of the witching hour, but they aren't allowed to occupy my mind for long before the tiny wakeman is sounding his shrill horn.

'When baby cries he wants something,' proclaims the currently fashionable bible of child-rearing with devastating perspicacity. Yes, but what, O Sage, O answer to the parents' prayer?

Well, there's a check list, if you've nothing better to run through at two in the morning.

'Food. Is he hungry?' He's guzzled so much that in the half-light, and delirious with tiredness, I imagine he's grown a snout.

'Wind?' He's just let out such a crack the neighbours have started knocking on the wall.

'Dry?' As snuff. I've had to take out a second mortgage to pay for all the disposable nappies.

'Comforting. Has he been comforted?' He couldn't have been more cosseted if he'd been the son of Henry VIII. He's been cuddled and kissed, cooed and wooed, loved and doved, coddled and mollycoddled. The list is enough to make non-parents throw up.

'But can he sense your exasperation? Is this what's making him unhappy?' Well, there you have me. Show me the parent who, after the umpteenth consecutive sleepless night, when having done everything in their mortal power to see that baby is warm and dry, fed and loved, and he still wails away all night like a tomcat, does not display some degree of exasperation and I'll show you someone who should be negotiating arms control agreements in Geneva, reasoning with Iran, in other words putting their prodigal powers of patience to the service of mankind.

'You may simply have a miserable child,' points out the child bible if all else fails to assuage his wails. A melancholy baby! Of Cerberus and blackest midnight born! Lying in his little cot reflecting on entropy, shaking his little fist at the sky and crying, 'Nought lasts!' I rule this one out, having only the sunniest disposition myself.

I have my own theories about what's wrong, and you don't have to be an expert on baby matters to come to the same conclusion. What baby wants is something to interest him. He doesn't know it's the middle of the night.

Besides, he's got this wonderful new brain which is capable of storing up more facts than the whole of the British Museum Reading Room, and it's crying out to be used.

To expect a new baby who has dozed all day, and doesn't do much in any case to get tired because his parents do everything for him, to sleep all night long is adult idiocy. He's bored, and unless someone gets up and does something interesting – like pull his hair out or jump up and down on the spot – he'll go on 'Wa Wa Wa-ing' all night long. In fact, it's precisely because Daddy does pull his hair out and shake his fist and pull amazingly funny faces at the same time as crying, 'Oh my God, why did we ever have him?', that it seems the best reason in the world for going on. It's better than listening to those stupid starlings shuffling around in the loft and the foundations settling.

There are certain more old-fashioned schools of thought who advocate ignoring a crying baby if there is nothing manifestly amiss. Buy some ear-plugs, take a bottle of Scotch to bed, sleep under the mattress, are all methods I have tried without success. But to the paediatric gurus of today, whose preposterous idealism goes unchallenged and makes all parents who fail to live up to it guilt-stricken and neurotic, the golden rule of parenthood is the same as that for a farmer who would lead a bull to market: always put him first. Baby's needs must come before yours. Build your life afresh around him. When he sleeps, you sleep. (Try explaining that one to the boss at work when he catches you with your head down at 3 o'clock in the afternoon.) When he calls, drop all else and run. Ignore the housework, your social life, your career, everything. Every minute spent with him is an investment in his future, his stability. You are laying foundations. If you skimp on love and care now, in later years the whole edifice may come tumbling down.

The most chilling implication of this infanticentric view of the universe, and the one that I find the most difficult to swallow, is that the parents' lives suddenly become unimportant. That we are little better than glorified potato plants, that once we have flowered we must just die off. The future rests with the little spuds wrapped in the dark protective soil beneath our withering leaves.

These melancholy conclusions are entirely the result of prowling the corridors at 2 and 3 o'clock in the morning with an animated bundle dribbling down my back.

As well as warping your personality, the disruption of one's sleep pattern from a normal healthy sine-curve to a series of fretful hiccups, does nothing to endear one to one's neighbours. Mid-morning callers who find you still in pyjamas and puke-ravaged bathrobe are inclined to believe you have joined the work-shy. Mothers-in-law are even worse. When they arrive for coffee expecting to be presented with a grandchild pink and powdered and clad in the Christopher Robin baby-suit they bought him for Christmas, and they find the house looking like a gipsy encampment, with parents stumbling around amongst the empty coffee-cups like the living dead, baby fast asleep for the first time since midnight, family bonds are stretched to breaking point.

'Well, I can't understand why he's not sleeping,' she says in censorship-laden tones as her eyes rake the domestic debris like a bulldozer. 'I never had this trouble.' Which means, of course, that it's all your fault. Tolerance being the first casualty of sleep-deprivation, there then follows a heated exchange on the rival merits of different generations' methods of child-rearing. It's suggested that we are over-stimulating baby: a nursery full of twisting mobiles, pop-up pictures, toys which squeak, rattle, light up and put themselves to bed at night, plus parents who gabble away at him like demented auctioneers for sixteen hours a day is thought to produce a kind of mental apoplexy. I try to explain that wrapping babies in swaddling clothes and sticking them in darkened rooms for six months like seed potatoes is no longer regarded as a good idea. Voices are raised and, of course, baby, itching for another fix of dangerous stimulation, wakes up and starts crying. He isn't going to miss the fun.

I peer at my watch. It's 11 a.m. This nightmare doesn't

end with daylight. King Herod has become a personal hero. I shall start an appreciation society, just as soon as I can get some sleep.

HAVE SON, WILL TRAVEL

We never bought him a pram, and I think there may be hell to pay for it later. You see, by not doing so we failed to register him in the consumer society. We deprived him of his first status object, and he may never recover. He may become a social outcast, like his father.

Brenda had her pram on order from the moment she knew she was pregnant. You see, you have to with a certain kind of pram whose name I shall not mention here for fear of doubling the waiting list. They're like Rolls-Royces and Eton, you have to put your name down months, years in advance. They glisten with chrome, and when the wheels go round they tick like a Swiss watch.

Gail has laid silk sheets and pillow cases in hers, and dresses little Jonathan in French designer baby-clothes. He doesn't seem to know because he still pukes and messes in them. I'd like to think he did know, and that every mess was a protest on behalf of all the starving poor who have only dust to cover their nakedness.

I'm not telling you this because we live in Sloane Street or Haslemere but because we live in the scrag-end of England where you really have to try to get noticed. Where we wave because we're drowning. This is where all the fancy prams go. They converge on the pavement outside the shops like a cavalcade of Fauntleroys. There's a hundred years' rent just in chrome and frilly lace.

Now don't get me wrong. I think it's nice to want the very best for your children. And I think new mums have every right to feel proud of themselves – bringing children into the world beats what any man can do by light years. It's just that I grow very uneasy about using babies as status symbols. I like to keep my hopes and aspirations to myself, not deck my baby out in them.

Yet, when I stepped out that first spring morning with my son stuck in a rucksack, a hole for his head and two for his tiny feet, with him clad in his cousin's cast-offs (turned ever such a bilious colour from all that biological washing powder eating at the stains), I was probably saying just as much about myself as all those turbo-buggies and designer nappies said about their owners.

The trouble in this self-conscious age is that you can't do or be anything without reflecting a well-worn image. It just happened that I was wearing wellies, a self-coloured Herdwick sweater, and a beard. Now I go out of my way to avoid labels. They once gave me a Radio 4 umbrella but I used it for forcing rhubarb. Yet my clothes and my backpack said it all. If I hadn't had a wash that morning I'd have looked definitely Stonehenge. Not Druid, but Wiltshire Wanderer by Greenham Common out of Hippie Convoy. Our young policemen are taught to recognise such types and spot-search them for unusual herbs. I reckon if I'd gone even anywhere near the prampushers, they'd have set upon me and battered me with their rattles for giving motherhood a bad name. Backpacks indeed!

But that back-pack was worth its weight in rusks. It gave me and my boy the freedom we needed to turn our backs on the pram-and-rattle race and keeping up with the Jonathans. We took to the hills and returned to nature, me and my squirming back-pack that dribbled down my neck and stuck sticky fingers in my eyes and ears. I took seven-league strides and sang like Tom Bombadil while he chuckled away like a mountain stream. He couldn't speak but he could hear, so I passed on everything I knew about skies and hills, birds and beasts. It was the best time of my life. Meanwhile he secretly shook off his boots and dropped his mittens so I had to trail back miles looking for them. He still remembers it, even if only for the supply of chocolates I took and we ate on the tops of hills amongst the skylarks and wheeling gulls.

Incurable romantic that I am, I'd like to think that I'd written something on the clean slate of his mind that will never be erased, something more enduring than a world bound and framed by a posh pram-hood. Who knows though? He could grow up hating the countryside. The March winds pinched his cheeks red raw, and sometimes he cried all the way home. And I felt guilty, foisting off my silly romanticism on a baby when he'd have been better off under a quilt being cooed at. He'll probably turn into a city slicker, only at peace in ferro-concrete, the sky trapped and tamed in the glass façade of an office block.

It's such a chancy business, influences. Take smacking. Do you smack naughty children? No one directly involved with children believes in smacking any more. So what do you do? My boy has learnt to spit. I don't know where he's learnt it from because his parents aren't in the habit of spitting at one another. If we say, 'No, you can't have a chocolate biscuit,' he vents his disappointment in spit. We try to reason, but you might as well spit against the wind as reason with a child of two. It's at this age that boys are possessed by a fury. It is, of course, the terrible twos. Ageing matrons with stolid upright sons who go to church will blanch as they recall it. If you, as the blessed parent of an angelic little girl, doubt that it exists, visit a few family restaurants and tea-rooms, or any public place which requires a modicum of civilisation from your child. There will be a suspicious lack of two-year-olds. This is because parents have tried, and it's just not worth it. You're better off staying at home than watching a plate of fish-fingers being flung at a stranger, or hearing the word Daddy inadvertently used when the screwdriver slipped being parroted non-stop throughout the meal. It's not worth having to chase them as they wriggle out of your grasp for the tenth time to seek out the most patent child-detester in the place to stand by their chair and try and wring a smile out of their crab-apple face with a thousand ghastly winsome antics. It's not worth a tantrum.

Nothing is worth a tantrum, not in public. Because when your child's face turns blue, and when he hurls himself around on the end of your hand like a rag doll, shrieking and choking, all because you have confiscated the sugar-tongs which he was using to pick his nose, people don't think, 'Oh, poor parent! Having to cope with that!'

No, they think it's your fault. Some weakness on your part. As if you'd never tried to control it. That's why I don't believe in smacking. Smack a child having a tantrum and you end up with a megatantrum. You see, he is quite simply possessed, and no power on earth short of exorcism will control him. The only safe way to deal with him is to ignore him. So you get scenes, which scandalise maiden aunts and grandmothers who have forgotten what it was all like, of two-year-old in the hyperstore pounding the floor because you decline to buy him a word-processor.

By far the most mixed blessing that has come the way of parents today is television. By 9.30 in the morning when we've built a shoe-box castle, baked a flour and water cake, done hand-dabbed paintings over half the kitchen wall, and been six times round the garden counting the remains of last night's squashed slugs, I'm crying out for *Playschool* to begin and someone else to take over. But children's television is plagued with pop videos: twilight worlds of alleyways with snarling vamps in crimson lipstick; a ghetto culture of prowling males in leather and rivets, thrusting and twitching to the howl of overstrung guitars. It's a pubescent dream, wet and shadowy, and my two-year-old watches it enthralled. At two! He should still be on Bambi and Paddington Bear. He's going to miss out on childhood and jump straight into the maelstrom of adolescence. No Enid Blyton. No *Wind in the Willows*. No Tom Bombadil. No more striding the high summer ridges on my back, his tiny hands reaching for the sky. I could weep. This age has murdered innocence. If it can't be marketed it's killed off. Like a lame calf.

Not long ago we went to visit relatives in a different part of the country: a mealy-mouthed little estate of thick hedges and hidden eyes. One day I set off with him in the back-pack for a walk. When I got back there was a knock on the door. It was a policeman.

'Can you prove that this is your child?'

'Do you want me to take a blood test?'

The strap under his chin kept every muscle in his face rigid. For all I know it kept his head on.

'We've had a call from a neighbour saying she saw this bearded stranger carrying off this small child in a back-pack.'

He made it sound like an offensive weapon.

'There's been a lot of this sort of thing recently.'

Afterwards, when I'd proved my innocence of child abduction, I wanted to napalm the estate. I wanted to take off with my son and his back-pack, and walk out of this world.

We would never have had this trouble if we'd bought a pram.

SMITH TAKES A BREAK

First broadcast October 1983

A RACE APART

For our trip to the August race meeting at York the sun never shone. We awoke to torrential rain and journeyed across the high Pennine moors in mist and grey cloud in which the sheep merged like sodden apparitions. Our spirits were low, and by Marston Moor, where Arthur began to conjure up images of headless Royalists bleeding into ditches, we dived into the nearest pub to chase away the dampness. Many of the punters must have had the same idea for the bar was full of snappy hats and macs with epaulettes and heads buried earnestly between the pages of the *Sporting Life*. The rain had caused consternation among the betting fraternity, changing the going from good to soft and confounding the pundits. We listened eagerly for names but made no headway: getting a good tip from a Yorkshireman is like prising a coin out of a dead man's hand. Arthur was very impressed by the price of the beer – only 51 pence a pint, and began to entertain a more charitable view of Yorkshiremen.

We ordered lunch and got something called a Cromwell Platter, full of ham and black puddings. It caused us to begin to entertain very Republican thoughts, which, like the weather, turned out to be very ominous.

The trouble really began to brew when we reached the course, having missed the first race due to the excellence and cheapness of the refreshment. We were both novices to racing, and Arthur's father, whose fist is as tight as chain-mail, had warned us beforehand about where we should go to watch it. I'd mentioned Tattersalls and he'd thrown a fit. 'You can't go there,' he foamed. 'It'll cost a fortune.' He told us to look for something called the Silver Ring. It would cost about 50 bob. The implication was clear: our station in life was around the 50-bob mark.

I was pondering upon this as we walked towards the turnstiles. On one side of us was a pavement strewn with rain-filled plastic trays in which pale chips and half-eaten sausages floated; on the other, a banked lawn aflame with multicoloured begonias. But as we stopped outside the entrance to the County Stand, like onlookers at a royal première, Lady Fate, as is her wont at race meetings, suddenly put in an appearance. A large and ostentatious limousine swept up, displacing a large quantity of gutter water all over Arthur's cavalry twills. Then, to add further humiliation, as he stooped to brush away the muddy droplets, the door was flung open sending him sprawling to the floor. Out breezed the occupants, pushed past us without an apology, and disappeared into the entrance to the County Stand.

So amazing was this behaviour we forgot all about Arthur's father's injunction and followed them in. If I was ever to rise above the 50-bob mark I must learn from the behaviour of my betters. Over the door read a warning: 'County Stand. Casual dress is prohibited. Persons dressed in a casual or offensive manner will be refused admission.'

I stood nervously before the nearest official, expecting him to grimace with disgust at any minute. 'Er, excuse me. Am I all right to come in?'

'Certainly, sir.'

I was encouraged. My natural aristocratic bearing was plain to see after all. 'What's offensive?' I asked him.

He looked puzzled. 'I beg pardon?'

'What is offensive dress?'

He thought for a minute. 'Oh, well, like not having a tie.'

He was a reasonable man, and as soon as he'd said it I

could see he knew how absurd it sounded. So he added, 'You know, an open shirt, and, er, dirty, and, er, looking like a tramp.' Then he leant forward confidentially, man to man, or should I say, gentleman to gentleman. 'You know, riff-raff.'

I nodded knowingly, and as I turned away he caught me by the arm and whispered, 'You can tek your tie off when you get inside, you know.'

Actually, I needed my tie to stop my head from falling off when I found out how much it cost to get into the County Stand. Sixteen pounds! Each! If Arthur's father found out that we'd paid £16 each just to get into the races, he'd never speak to us again. He'd disown us as traitors to our class – the 50-bobs. All around us the cash desk crackled like a bush fire with people handing over crisp new banknotes. Arthur and I counted out our coppers in a corner. After we paid, we both felt remorseful.

You can't spend half a lifetime rolling empty toothpaste tubes and leaving sauce bottles upside down in the cupboard to squeeze the last bit out of them, and then go off and spend £16 – £16 – getting into the races. I felt terrible. It was my first big test and I'd failed it. I was a 50-bob chap after all, and my 50-bob soul cried out in dismay.

Arthur was more philosophical. We were here to observe the English social scene and we couldn't do it properly from a 50-bob enclosure full of tramps with no ties on. We were paying for knowledge. You could probably get a grant for this kind of thing somewhere. We'd keep our badges and write off when we got back home. Maybe the Open University.

Our badges were green and were very important. They had a little string and you had to fasten them about your person, so that everybody knew you weren't riff-raff. (Arthur said they were green to show how daft we were to pay £16.) Not that there was any doubting that we were amongst a different class of person as soon as we stepped inside the County Stand. It was a good job we were under cover and the place wasn't full of puddles like outside or we'd have both been drowned. As it was, they had to make do with pushing us aside. At first you might think it's rudeness to behave as though other people don't exist, to be trampled on if they get in the way or ignored if they should suddenly drop dead at your feet. Nothing of the kind. After standing at one doorway for a full five minutes trying to get through only to be pushed aside by countless waves of tweeds and cashmere coats and voices crying, 'I'd love one,' and 'Really?', I suddenly realised they weren't being rude at all. It was simply that Arthur and I were invisible. Despite our badges. Who blames the car driver who pulps the humble hedgehog that scuttles into his path? They live in different worlds. One's horizon is the gutter, the other's the stars. And so with men. Arthur and I were being made to feel humbly conscious of the gulf.

What other privileges did our £16 bestow? Well, I was able to order a gin and tonic from a makeshift bar. It was served in a plastic container and I was asked to help myself to ice and lemon. When I pointed out that there were no tongs in the silver ice bucket, I was told that you never get germs in ice. It was a polite way of saying that people in the County Stand didn't have germs. We could have ventured into a stark dining room and lunched off roast beef and frozen vegetables, followed by strawberries and rather watery-looking cream. We could have sat with a bottle of claret on the table and looked bored like a lady we saw with a bright red pill-box hat stuffed with ostrich feathers, which made her look for all the world as though she was on fire, but determined not to make a fuss about it. We could have used a toilet which contained eau de lavender, silver-backed hairbrushes, and face-powder in a cut-glass bowl – only it turned out to be the ladies, which starstruck Arthur wandered into by accident. But what really made us feel that our investment had been a wise one was when we strayed beyond some swing-doors and, horrors! A Dantean nightmare! Smoke-filled shadows lit by the harsh glare of strip-lighting. Tables crammed with beer and bodies, beer and bellies. And denim, unspeakable denim, everywhere. The smell of wet dog and mouse's cage hung over everything. We shuddered. It was the 50-bob bar. We were back where we belonged.

It had all been a dream, the cashmere and the claret, the Oxford voices and ostrich feathers. I felt in my pocket for my £16. But no, the money had gone, and there was my green badge, its corner beginning to curl in the warm fug of beer and cigarette smoke. I thought I saw calloused hands reaching to pluck it from me, social envy burning in every glance. We turned and fled, making the quantum leap back into the County Stand and sinking with relief into the soft pile of the carpeted corridor.

Our social identity crisis was deepening, and when Arthur was struck violently on the head by a passing champagne cork we decided it was time to concentrate on the racing. We invested what meagre resources still remained on the big race of the afternoon. Outside on the terraces the Knavesmire is grey; clouds lour upon the houses of York. The rain, no respecter of class, streams down on rich and poor alike. But in the County Stand the umbrellas are thick and plentiful. We try to squeeze between them for a view of events, but they keep close ranks in the County Stand. I end up with the water from the nearest umbrella trickling down my neck. I've time to observe that the lovely boxes of geraniums which adorn the stand stop short of the 50-bob enclosure. An appreciation of beauty clearly does not extend to the riff-raff.

The loudspeaker announces that they're under starter's orders. We peer into the mists while binoculars are raised around us. I can't see a thing. Neither can a lady behind. 'I say there,' she cries. 'You with the umbrella. Do you mind!' Confidence, I observe, is the keynote of social superiority, as the offending gamp is swiftly lowered. We suffer in silence as more deflected rainwater begins to fill my shoe. They've reached the five-furlong mark and we recognise the names of the horses we've backed. Four furlongs and they start to challenge. Three, and we spot them for the first time: an untidy knot of straining necks and drilling hooves. Two furlongs and the crowd bursts into life. Our horses have hit the front. I've stopped breathing and my heart's running its own race up into my mouth.

With a drum of hooves they flash past the post. Arthur and I look at each other. We've both gone white. We've got first, second, and third!

We reinvest our winnings on the next two races, determined to recoup our entrance fee. We lose. I risk what's left on the next race, putting the money on to win. The horse comes third.

Dejectedly we wander over to the winners' enclosure. It's our first close-up of a racehorse. They're steaming in the damp air, the inside of their flanks soapy with foam. Nostrils flare, eyes bolt uneasily. We sense the strangeness, the primitiveness of the creatures. Then they're gone, whisked away like film stars, and we're left with the human bloodstock: confident men in pale raincoats with creamy pampered complexions, their women tall, slim, expensively groomed appurtenances, baring rows of even white teeth. Someone points out a lord, tottering down from his special box. It's rumoured he had four figures on the last race. Did he win? His face gives nothing away but the strain of the battle against decrepitude. Arthur and I turn to leave, hands in our empty pockets.

Arthur suddenly announces that instead of going straight home he wants to visit the Minster. We stand outside the west door staring morosely up at the ruined faces of saints. What does he want from all this, I wonder? Is he hankering for the Middle Ages, where no amount of green badges would give you ideas above your station? Inside the Minister we are met by another notice: Admission is free, but a gift of at least 75 pence from each visitor would be appreciated. We shuffle guiltily past without removing our hands from our pockets and into the solemn Gothic forest of stonework. We passed marble tombs with sleeping effigies of lords and archbishops, and a screen of kings with golden crowns, all looking as if they'd lost at the races. We sat down in front of the great east window, under the pewter light, feeling the solace of ancient stonework.

'Who am I?' whispered Arthur at last.

Like the tracery in the vaulted roof our thoughts met.

'You mean 50-bob, or green badge?'

41

'Yes,' said Arthur, 'that'll do.'

'Neither,' I said. 'We're just ourselves.'

'That'll do, as well,' said Arthur, happy at last. 'By the way, don't you keep some spare money in the glove compartment of the car?'

'By gum, yes,' I said.

So we had tea at Rooney's fish bar, taking care to put our green badges back on before we stepped inside.

OVER WORDSWORTH'S GRAVE

'He's trailing his little clouds of glory,' I observed, as we watched a small child trying to put his foot into a milk-jug in this rather superior little tea-shop in Ambleside. You could tell the shop was superior because they served things like ginger preserve and something called Original Cumberland Rum Nicky, ample evidence of which was to be seen smeared across the infant's purple face. Having been thwarted in his attempts to put the milk-jug on his foot, he was venting his rage by screaming his head off and pounding the bone china plates with his little fist. As befits parents who frequent genteel tea-shops, they were ignoring their child's tantrum with saint-like fortitude.

'He was quite mad, you know,' I went on.

'Who?' grunted Arthur, who had piled so much damson preserve and whipped cream onto his scone that he could no longer get it into his mouth without depositing most of the cream on his nose-end.

'Wordsworth, of course,' I replied, astonished now to see the child lift the teapot and try to drink from the spout while his parents appeared to be deeply engrossed in Beatrix Potter's *Life and Times of Peter Rabbit*. 'He goes on to say that children are "mighty prophets" and "seers blessed".'

Arthur opened his mouth like a hippopotamus to dispatch the scone. He took a little while to digest this.

'He's probably right,' he said finally. It was my turn to be open-mouthed.

'I mean,' explained Arthur, 'it's the little brat's way of protesting at all this lot.'

By 'all this lot', Arthur was presumably referring to the Lake District we'd just observed. We'd traversed Cumbria's answer to the Golden Mile, the shore of Windermere from Bowness to Ambleside. This is the great highway to the glorious mountains and yet it's as twee and silly as a schoolgirl's bedroom. Take Bowness, full of gift shops smelling of pot pourri and herbal bath soaps. The different uses to which nature can be put in the interests of commerce would have surprised that inveterate inspector of small celandines, Wordsworth himself. Elderflower talc. Myrtle skin cream. They're even taken to cosily packaging the geological aeons by printing 'This is made from natural slate over 500 million years old' on the mantelpiece bric-à-brac of pen-holders and ashtrays. I'm sure it's far more crass to defile stone of this age with etchings of cuddly rabbits and carthorses than to tout the honest vulgar trash of the Blackpool gift shops that turns up on the shelf next to it.

I wonder how Wordsworth's shocking solemnity would have dealt with: 'Fun Blood' ('Looks like blood, flows like blood!'), 'Bang Chewing Gum' ('Shock your friends'), or 'The Tellie Brick', a foam construction which urges you to 'Buy one, chuck it tonight!' (He'd have probably grown to like that one.) I doubt if he'd have written an

Ode to a Muppet Stick, though I did notice that they were selling opium incense sticks, something he might have been tempted to buy for chum Coleridge. But while he may not have laughed too heartily, I suspect that a man who tarried with Leech Gatherers and the like might have had more time for the vulgar gew-gaws of Bowness and Windermere than its plethora of over-priced middle-class stuff. Sheep-skin shops selling leather pants at a price that would have kept the entire nineteenth-century Lakeland workforce in moleskins for life. We counted enough wine cradles and Ali Baba baskets to fill every semi-detached from Nuneaton to Crewkerne.

To complete Arthur's Wordsworthian education we decided to pay a visit to Dove Cottage. Unfortunately we confused it with Rydal Mount, where Wordsworth lived later in life and ultimately died. We were soon pounced on by one of those tremendously eager and knowledgeable ladies which the National Trust keeps in linen chests in all its stately and historical homes. They usually sit knitting at a window seat wearing pearls and looking like the owner, wigging at your conversation and waiting for you to make some mistake about identifying a picture or piece of furniture; then they'll leap out and regale you with a detailed account of the house and all its contents and try to sell you a life membership to the Trust.

We were rather late, as we generally are, putting visits to tea-shops and other watering holes before cultural excursions, so we were whisked inside and made to stand in the breakfast room while a quorum of other luckless visitors was found. I tried to explain that I just wanted to wander around, but it was too late. Two Americans were found in the garden trying to prise lumps of stone from the walls to take home to Kansas City and dragged inside, and our guide launched into a history of the house long before Wordsworth came to live there. Arthur got very melancholy very quickly. It was all the heavy oak furniture and bare boards and boring Victoriana. There was Wordsworth's sofa, presumably the one on which he used to lie in vacant and pensive mood thinking about all those daffodils. It's a horrible black thing, covered in some stuff that looked like insulation tape. You just couldn't imagine anyone having sublime thoughts surrounded by so much dourness. And it was all a bit sinister, like fragments of a nightmare. There were bits of Dora's dolls' tea-set, and some frightful winter houseboots thought to have belonged to Dorothy – more like Miss Havisham – made of white kid with silk ribbons, narrow and faded: prettified decay that somehow reminded you of toadstools. It was all too much for Arthur, and with the black cloud hanging over him he announced that he was off to see the room where Wordsworth died. We trailed up some creaky stairs, the air heavy with polish and Wordsworthian gravity. We passed more of the wretched memorabilia. One stark standchair was simply labelled 'A Wordsworth Chair'.

We trailed into the deathroom, William and Mary's. They had single beds – which comes as no surprise – and just down the corridor, only a short sigh away, dear sister Dorothy's room. All the other Wordsworths hung about the bedroom: grandfathers, sons, grandsons; what a stern, grim, poker-faced lot, lowering from the walls in sepia solemnity. All in on the act; made famous by the gene that glamorised the daffodil and glorified the empty slopes of Skiddaw. There was younger brother Chris, Master of Trinity, an unrelenting, thin-lipped hymnwriter. There were no echoes in the room, only the leaden gaze of the Wordsworth tribe. 'Cor, look at the hooters!' observed Arthur. The Wordsworth nose must have been as impressive a spectacle as any jutting crag or rocky promontory that Willie chose to write of.

I went to the window for some air, to try and get some idea of what inspiration must have filtered through and lit up the shadows of this house. This was the same window through which the giant soul must have winged on its way to join the rocks and stones and trees. Outside, down below, a tourist was busy concealing an empty Coca Cola can in a laurel hedge. A small child, chocolate-coloured in hue, was having yet another tantrum. I marvelled that Wordsworth could have such universal appeal. In the foyer the guides to the house were translated into every tongue: Urdu, Korean, Esperanto, Hindi, Bengali. The thought of 'The Prelude' rendered in Esperanto sent us scuttling for the car. We could just make Dove Cottage before they closed. Perhaps the spirit of a more youthful and carefree Wordsworth was in residence there.

Our culture is being packaged as neatly and impregnably as a carton of tea-bags these days. With 12 million trophy-hunting overseas visitors a year, it's no wonder we need to put barbed wire round Stonehenge and charge £1.50 to enter Dove Cottage.

We were too late for the conducted tour. There was no question of slipping in like some late-comer to church. There was the notice: Next admission, 9.30 a.m. We'd have to sleep it out under the stars on Rydal Fell. I tried the door but it was locked. From within I could hear the reverential tones of the guide discussing the Wordsworths' plumbing arrangements. I peered in through a window. More shadows, but full of people, hushed, pilgrims at a shrine. It felt and reeked of school, pious and out of proportion. OK, what did you do to change the world, Wordsworth? You've filled the gift shops in Ambleside and made us all hang pretty calendars with views of Grasmere on our walls. But what good does it do, all this nature worship? I shook my fist at the maddeningly obdurate hills, made of slate 500 million years old. Go on, do something for me, instead of making me feel inadequate and insignificant!

Arthur, sensing some sort of crisis brought on by what he called the Wordsworm, announced that he thought there was a party going on in one of the buildings opposite. People were going in and out, actually smiling. I swore I heard the sound of laughter and glasses chinking. Alas, it was a sort of delirium brought on by the Wordsworm. It turned out to be a library full of the great bard's Niagaran outpourings being conscientiously visited by the endless river of tourists.

It's undoubtedly the middle classes for whom the discovery of the English countryside has done most good. And an honest, decent sort of person they are. You find them everywhere in the Lakes: ensconced in their garden chairs at the boot of the car with salad stuff in margarine cartons; or on the fells with bristly knees and Alfred Wainwright in their pockets. Unfortunately, however, decent folk can be rather dull, and the annual Grasmere sports, held within a javelin's throw of Dove Cottage, turned out to be the epitome of that dullness. It was all so quiet. A couple of thousand people, but all so subdued, as if people were upset, unnerved by the silent watchfulness of the surrounding hills. Or perhaps it was the spirit of Wordsworth, damp and resentful as a wet August day, hating the intrusion. We tried to analyse what was wrong. It was all decent and tasteful. There were no vulgar side shows, no crass commercialism, no touts, louts, loblolly men or loafers. There was no slurping, slopping plastic-cup-filled beer-tent for tippling, tipsy farmers with their braces on and flat caps pulled down over their red faces. Nothing to embarrass decent folk. Even the children were well-behaved and only one or two tantrums were being thrown. There was just the middle classes, the country-loving, corn-dolly, hand-carved walking stick, Ordnance Survey, jam and scone-loving middle classes. There they were politely, restrainedly watching the spectacle in the sun; watching the running and the jumping and the Cumberland wrestlers locked together like stags in long johns. In fact, it was all as flat and lifeless as a kipper fillet. The only time the crowd showed any passion was when the man on the loudspeaker announced that someone had gone and left his dog in the car without the window open. Then, such a murmur of indignation rose up towards the hills, you felt that if they'd got hold of the scoundrel they'd have lynched him on the spot.

I suppose we've drained all the virility out of the countryside by turning it into a spectacle, a prospect from a car window, a gift shop full of bogus rustic crafts. I suppose we're not much further on than they were before Wordsworth arrived and went ranting and booming about the hills. I suggested to Arthur that we should go and buy a rope and hang there from some rock-face until we'd driven the smell of pot pourri from our nostrils. Arthur thought it was a good idea in theory. But wasn't there a rather nice little tea-shop we hadn't tried back in Ambleside?

We ambled back to the car park, passing a man in a deckchair reading a paper: 'Midnight terror of boy hooked on video!' A party led by a formidable-looking German woman with a mouth like a pike charged past us towards Dove Cottage. An American asked Arthur's permission to take a picture of Grasmere.

'What do you think of it all?' I asked him.

'Gee, swell. Real swell.'

'Absolutely,' we agreed, and off we went for tea.

THE NAVEL OF THE NORTH

Blackpool is like the sea: full of change, but always the same. This season on the promenade they've parked a Tornado fighter-bomber which the kids can scramble over, their fingers sticky with rock and candyfloss. Next to it there's a Bloodhound ground-to-air missile, its wicked snout pointing right at Butlin's holiday camp. (I wonder if the people who set it up once had a rotten holiday there?) A pram-pushing man wearing a British Heart Foundation T-shirt studies an ejector seat. His T-shirt reads: 'It's great to be alive!'

Just what the RAF is playing at, staging an exhibition like this in the Fun Capital of the North, I don't know. But Blackpool is renowned for its lack of subtlety. It's one of its charms. Down on the front, the tide's in; a slurry of brown water lapping against the prom. Everybody's retreated onto the concrete, treating it with all the lack of ceremony of their own backyard. Large ladies sunbathe in their bras. Everybody's eating.

People eat everywhere and anywhere in Blackpool. A

Scotsman in a ridiculous tartan hat with a yellow bobble is slumped in a deckchair, his stomach overlapping the edges, spooning fish and chips into his mouth with a wooden fork. Next to him his wife reads the *Sun*, her lips moving to the words like a child at junior school. There are donkey droppings everywhere, and skinny kids with

goosepimples wrapped in towels. No one has any self-consciousness in Blackpool. They let it all hang out.

Not many yards from the missiles and the nuclear bomber is the cenotaph. There's an RAF brass band playing. Trombones flash gold in the sun, matching the gold braid on the bandsmen's epaulettes. People sit and lie around the grass. Two large ladies straight out of a Bamforth's postcard lie flat on their backs, their bosoms pointing skywards, missiles of their own. Blackpool may well be a parody of itself with bulges and bottoms and fish and chips, but feelings, too, stir, deep down, like the tide beneath the stanchions of the pier. There's a strong but dead tradition of good music in the working-class North: oratorios in church halls, brass bands in parks – and the race memory is stirred. People keep arriving, drawn to the sound, faint smiles playing on their faces. It's not the muzak that paints the walls of all the bars and cocktail lounges, but real music, which moves breasts which some, especially from politer places, see as half savage. A baby beats time in his pram. When a piece comes to an end, people clap, enthusiastically, appreciatively.

It's a rare nuance that's easily buried in the belly of big brash Blackpool, the navel of the North.

Across the way, just at the entrance to the North Pier, there's entertainment of a different sort going on in the Merrie England Bar. This is a fine piece of rustic affectation, the Merrie England Bar. You can eat your ploughman's lunch under a huge beech tree, and you'll never know the chagrin of Autumn, because the tree is made entirely of plastic. Its only signs of age, the slow accretions of dust on its leaves and beerstains down its trunk. On the wall is a huge flannelgraph of a village scene with merry milkmaids dancing with their swains. All it lacks is birdsong, but this is made up for by the bleep and whine of the space-invader machines that line the rustic stockade that serves for a wall. One small child is so struck by the beauty of this country scene that the moment he comes through the door with his parents, he lets out a pitiful howl, which never ceases until he's dragged away again.

Meanwhile, deep inside the bar, far from natural daylight, an even more pitiful sound is heard. An impromptu talent competition is under way, where the audience, emboldened by lager and blackcurrant, is encouraged to stand up and have a go. A small Welshman is singing 'I believe' with all the musical accomplishment of a werewolf baying at the moon. He's followed by Mandy and Trisha from London shrilling on about California for a full ten minutes. They are perfectly at ease with their own tonal deafness. 'We are all just prisoners here', they sing, and a man at the table next to us lunges for the daylight in a sudden bid to escape. But when they're finished, the applause is unstinted. What the audience lacks in criticalness they make up for in generosity. They're all on holiday and out to have a good time, and the generosity and warmth spread over all and everything without discrimination.

You feel that if the Tornado aircraft were suddenly to take off to repel the oncoming might of Soviet Russia, they'd all order another round of drinks and welcome the next act. As it is, there are no more volunteers. Unfortunately, Arthur chooses this moment to get up and go to the loo. The man at the microphone asks for a big round of applause and Arthur, red-faced and floundering, finds himself being propelled towards the stage by a lot of helpful hands. I have to rush to the rescue. Pressing my pocket radio to my ear I stand up. 'Fire!' I cry. 'He's got to go. We're firemen, you know.' Arthur follows me out to a further generous round of applause. 'You're doing a grand job,' cries one old dear after us.

Next door is an amusement arcade. The noise from the machines is appalling, a cross between bedlam and a tropical rain forest in the mating season. The electronic machines chatter and scream in a barrage of video starburst and inter-galactic gunfire. It's easy now to see why the RAF are parked outside. They're hoping to recruit a few Buck Rogers. Kids these days show remarkable co-ordination. Programmed by television advertising, they're all reflexes and no thought – just what you need to fly a Jaguar and wipe out humanity. I have a go at racing a Grand Prix car around Silverstone. I crash thirteen times and wipe out the entire opposition. It's the lowest score ever recorded. An orang-outang could have done better. All the games these days are of the space-invader, video-screen type: games of skill rather than avarice, which I suppose is a hopeful sign. They retain a few of the old slot-machines and this is where the older people come.

One old lady, clutching her purse tightly, shuffles towards a machine. Her white hair is permed close and tight as coral. Lips clamped purposefully together, she drops her money onto the shelf of brown coins. They're nudged imperceptibly forward but nothing falls. She should have known: money sticks to money. She turns away muttering a curse. We follow her. This is our generation now. We've been superseded and are as obsolete as the cannon-ball. I can't even follow the instructions on these video games, never mind play them. Darth Vader has people like me for breakfast.

We wander through into the cafeteria; out to grass. This is our scene, amongst the old ladies sitting in their woollen topcoats dispatching haddock and chips with the mechanical relentlessness of the tide gnawing at the North Shore. You can look out onto the pier. This is where the old are set out in rows of forms and deckchairs like exhibits in a museum. There's a story of such usage in each face and body, a living history. There are miners with coal dust worn into their faces, ladies with legs swathed in crepe, bandaged like war-heroes. Theirs has been life's war: having babies, standing eight hours a day at a machine, grovelling at a coal-seam. Their wounds are varicose veins, rheumatism, bronchitis. One man, maybe once a clerk, has a battery of pens in his blazer pocket. He wipes the water out of his eye with a cotton handkerchief woven in Burnley forty years ago. Someone on the same pier probably wove it. They have a common background, the same roots, the same experiences, and despite a cool and nagging breeze the atmosphere's warm with shared memories. Life's worked them hard and they've come to Blackpool for some fun, even if it only means sitting in a deckchair all day swapping memories of monkey nuts and the one-and-nines at the old Alhambra.

'Salt of the earth,' whispers Arthur and turns away with a bit of water in his eye.

Suddenly the reveries are shattered. The air is torn apart and gulls and pigeons scattered everywhere. Old hearts lurch and walking frames clatter to the floor. Children scream and point upwards and ice creams go slithering off their cornets. It's the moment they've all been dreading in the town hall, and for the next fifteen minutes they'll be biting their nails and chain-smoking, praying that the £50 million pounds worth of insurance they've taken out won't be needed. Out of the grey sea-fret the Red Arrows have burst, racing towards the Tower and peeling off at the last sickening second. The whole prom erupts in oohs and ahs. Smoke and the smell of aviation fuel fill the air. The birds hide under the pier amongst the undemonstrative barnacles. The rest of us gawp and gasp and fail to grasp the speed of progress. There it was, gone!

In Blaekpool, old and new exist happily together in the timeless pursuit of fun. A man steps onto the pier who is straight out of a war-time newsreel. His hair cut two inches above his ears, his baggy grey suit, even his head has a 1940s shape. He smokes his cigarette until there's nothing left, without burning his fingers. He overtakes a party of punks: orange hair aflame above earrings and dayglo green sweaters.

'I never kept a pair o' shoes more than six months,' one of them boasts. They all look in at the joke shop; at Betty Boobs, the dirty nose-drop ('Watch the disgusted looks!'). And they all laugh at the jokes: pyjamas – articles placed in bed in case of fire; brassières: a device for making mountains out of molehills. The humour, like the fun, is very basic.

But it doesn't need to be. At the same time as they're laughing at the smut on the pier, the North Shore's answer to the Von Trapps are performing their own graceful version of the Hokey-Cokey under the gold rococo ceiling and glittering chandeliers of the Tower Ballroom. From the age of two to forty-two, all in shining gold dance shoes, this family of Terpsichoreans are bringing delighted ripples of applause from the people at their tables drinking Cinzano and lemonade. Against a painted backcloth of scenes of Sorrento, the giant Wurlitzer thunders away. At the end, still trembling along, it melts magically into the floor, and – hey presto! – is born again, with a different player and a different tune. The Von Trapps retire and single couples take to the floor in good old-fashioned contact dancing – none of this squirming about on your own, but arms stuck out like bowsprits, gliding along like tea-clippers to strains from the Vienna Woods.

We finished off by going up the Tower, a perilous journey for the faint of heart, cramped inside a swaying, rickety lift. You pass more rivets than there are stars in the sky or fish in the sea. Licked by the salty tongue of the wind for a century, the girders are worn and flaky. We shudder to a stop at the top and step tentatively out. From the air Blackpool is all Accrington brick and Welsh slate. The sea is Welsh slate too, but grained, with flecks of gulls weaving along its surface. Out towards the Isle of Man is a broad silver highway lit by the hazy sun. White waves trail inshore like rayfish, and the wrinkled skin of the sea is endlessly stretching over the sand and back, leaving silky patterns. The donkeys are back in business now that the tide is retreating, and you can hear the plaintive tinkling of their bells through the distant roar of the traffic journeying down to St Anne's for afternoon tea in its posh hotels.

Arthur's writing something down on a piece of paper near the parapet and a man, thinking it's a farewell note, rushes up to him and tells him not to do it. God loves everyone, he says, and hands him a leaflet entitled 'God's Plan'. Later we look through it, but Arthur's name is not mentioned.

'What were you writing?' I asked.

'I've got this idea for a book,' he said. 'It's about these people who steal a Tornado and threaten to blow up the House of Commons unless Blackpool's allowed to take over the running of the country.'

It would make a rotten book, but it's a good idea. If we let Blackpool take over, there'd be no more national debt, lots of self-confidence and generosity of spirit, and fish and chips for everybody. We could all do worse than rediscover some of the vulgar vigour of Blackpool. Life would be a lot simpler, and much more fun.

FOREIGN PARTS

From the viewpoint of The Poet and Peasant Working Men's Club the word 'abroad' means different things to different people. To one of us it means sun-kissed beaches, the unending vista of supine sun-worshippers broken only by a vision of Aphrodite playing topless beach tennis. To another it is those carefree après-sol moments within the soothing shade of a taverna, life hazily viewed through the bottom of a glass, the walls spinning gently to the beat of disco music. But so rare is it to find anything which appeals so much to the popular imagination about foreign holidays between these poles of sex and cheap alcohol that when Arthur put down his holiday brochure with the dreamy look of a Cortez laying down his telescope and whispered, 'The Cradle of Civilisation', not a drop of Butterworth's best bitter passed anyone's lips for a full minute.

That Arthur had been persuaded to pick up a continental holiday brochure was in itself a remarkable thing. In thirty-seven years the annual migratory instinct had never exerted sufficient power to take him further than the Yorkshire Dales or the Lake District. You could tell there was something inimical to foreign parts about Arthur right away, even without mentioning French Golden Delicious or apartheid. It was his colour. Arthur's native hue is deathly pale, like limestone touched by moonlight, or forced rhubarb roots. All the broiling sun of the summer of 1976 did nothing to Arthur's immense pallor but encourage the appearance of a scattering of ginger freckles. He was clearly not fashioned for foreign travel.

'Greece?' I cried. 'But we'll have to fly there!'

But Arthur ignored my trepidation. He was under the spell of Attica. 'Icarus,' he murmured, and I knew there was no turning back.

While Icarus' flight to the sun was accompanied by great hubris, mine was marked by an abject and cringing misery. My aversion to flight is nine parts cowardice, but the tenth is made up of good sense born from experience. There was the time I once stood at the end of a runway watching an RAF flying display. I struck up a conversation with the man next to me, who seemed to know a great deal about the planes. 'Do you fly them?' I asked ingenuously. 'Not blooming likely,' he cried. 'I service 'em.' This conversation kept sidling into my brain with all the dark menace of a hired assassin as I gazed out at the engine revving up on the tarmac. The rivets looked as if they could pop at any moment like cheap waistcoat buttons.

But the worst moment of all was when the chief stewardess cheerfully introduced the pilot. 'Your Captain, Captain Le Jetbash.' I couldn't believe my ears. Captain Le Jetbash. How many aeroplanes had he reduced to the state of battered stockcars?

Having reconciled myself to death I began to look around at my fellow passengers with the eye of a director in a disaster movie. What would they be like when word got round that a deadly virus had overtaken the flight crew? It was obvious that I'd got the hysterical one next to me, the one who would try to open the emergency doors at 30,000 feet. You could tell by the way he was already halfway through his bottle of duty-free Scotch and humming 'Nearer my God to Thee'. I quaked in an unhappy heap, as we roared down the runway. Trying to think of Biggles didn't help. That was the trouble. I wouldn't even have trusted Biggles, if he'd been in charge instead of Captain Le Jetbash. I have to check all the wheel-nuts when the car comes back from the garage.

The next four hours I spend in a limbo of terror. Looking out of the window doesn't help. The wing is wobbling and shaking like a dipso's hand. I know nothing about aircraft, but the phrase 'metal fatigue' rises out of my subconscious like a kraken. The cabin staff's valiant attempts to still the trepidation of the nervous by handing out foodstuffs locked inside maddeningly impregnable cling-film work only briefly. The sight and smell of a steamed sausage has me fumbling for the paper bag in the seat in front. At 33,000 feet Arthur is a tower of strength and tries to laugh me out of it.

He thinks he's brought a cat flea and wonders whether to write to the Guinness Book of Records when he gets back – the highest jumping flea in the world!

I stare morosely out at the alto-cumulus below and wonder when the sallow-skinned man opposite, who's clearly an international terrorist, is going to leap up and tell us about the bomb. Fear is debilitating; it drains every ounce of colour out of life. At six miles high I meet my true self for the first time: a snivelling wretch buoyed up by mere words that seem now as empty as air. It's me, not the man in the next seat, who would trample on women and children to save his own miserable skin; for the man next door, the whisky bottle empty, sleeps like a babe, his mouth wide open, a peaceful snore wheezing round his tonsils. Arthur catches me feeling for the seams in the porthole and, sensing an impending crisis, lays down his edition of *Jason and the Argonauts* and arranges with the stewardess for us to visit the flightdeck. I meet Captain Le Jetbash and am amazed. Instead of crouching over the controls like Barry Sheene, he sits, a model of cool and impeccable professionalism, surveying his instruments like a lesser deity. Slowly I begin to breathe more freely. The Aegean spreads below us, the wine-dark, the mackerel-crowded seas. Beyond, the shimmering Cyclades. All is well, and Icarus, having skirted the sun, glides smoothly down into the warm brown arms of Attica.

If Greece be the cradle of civilisation, I can report that despite the passing centuries the child has still not grown up, but toddles boisterously about in a state of rude and noisy health. Our hotel was in Glyfada, a coastal resort near Athens. It must be the noisiest place on earth.

The moment we stepped into the taxi at the airport the driver set off like a vengeful harpy, determined to strike terror and remorse into the breasts of all other road-users. This is clearly Article One of the Greek Highway Code. Since Article Two seems to be: 'Treat a red light with all the seriousness you would a stranger who asks you for 10,000 drachmas,' the resultant drama on the roads is drama as only the Greeks know it. But death and severe mutilation – which we witnessed on several occasions – is treated with the utmost casualness, the only emotion being the irritation of other road-users at being held up while the bits and pieces are being removed. Horns are sounded in a crescendo of impatience – a sort of maniacal Last Post to dispatch the departed soul on his way into the next world.

Of course, our hotel was right next to one such Stygian highway, where the sound of horns and burning tyres and the screams of the maimed continued unabated day and night. But the noise from this was nothing compared to that which beat down from the skies. The tour operators in their brochure failed to mention that Glyfada is under the flight-path into Athens airport. Every several minutes, day and night, mighty aircraft pass overhead at 250 feet, rendering all human communication beyond a feeble croak of despair impossible. There was simply no refuge from this barrage of decibels. To try and get some sleep Arthur took his snorkel and sat under water in the sea. We slept not a wink for five days and nights, for even when the last plane had flown over, the last car roared off into the night, when the hotel bar had at last disgorged its rowdy revellers, when the last dry cicada had finally itched itself to sleep in the orange trees; even then we were not done with Glyfada's torment of noise.

For then it was the turn of the dogs, of Cerberus and his midnight chums. For Greek dogs sleep all day under trees in mangy heaps, only to come out at night to yap and yelp outside hotel windows. Each day from the beach Arthur collected many a hundredweight of rocks and stones in readiness for these nightly visitors. And every night, at 3 a.m., he would burst out onto the balcony like Hercules with the shirt of Nessus upon him, and pelt these curs with missiles. The final straw came on the sixth day, at dawn, when the cries of smitten whelps retreating into the distance were drowned by the roar of a mechanical excavator arriving to complete the unfinished swimming pool beneath our window. We packed our bags, and left civilisation for a remote fishing village on the other coast.

Like our swimming pool, there is much unfinished building work in Greece. For a while, this led me to the view that the Acropolis is not a ruin after all but merely yet another Greek building which never got finished. The explanation for this dilatoriness lies in the somewhat less than vigorous approach to life – excluding driving, of course – of the modern Greek. Arthur tells me that the expression is 'laid back'. If you journey to Greece expecting to find in the people anything of the dynamism that in the fifth century BC brought us democracy, art, literature, and everything we hold so dear, if only because it grows so rare these days, you will be disappointed. The modern Greek resembles his ancient city-state counterpart much as a cheese slice resembles a piece of blue Stilton. Maybe it's the heat. Wading around in an atmosphere that resembles warm milk all day replaced many of my finer thoughts with images of chilled beer by the drayload.

The only strong evidence of the Greeks' classical ancestry was to be found on the beaches, where Narcissus is still alive and well and contemplating his own loveliness in self-satisfied rapture.

Still, Arthur was determined to capture as much of the glory that was Greece that is still left, and he bundled me onto a coach for Cape Sounion and the Temple of Poseidon. After a three-hour nightmare journey we arrived to find we had just fifty minutes to survey the ongoing building works which began in the Fourth Millennium. Perched on a promontory, beetling above the churning Aegean, it is the archetypal Greek ruin. Unfortunately, our arrival coincided with the arrival of twenty other like coaches, that promptly jettisoned their cargo and left them to swarm over the venerable marbles like ants over a discarded Chinese takeaway. We never got a chance to catch the atmosphere. Arthur was so disappointed that when our guide announced that most of the columns of the temple had been stolen by pirates, he observed loudly that the Greeks seemed to be in the habit of losing their marbles. The afternoon ended with Arthur's hat blowing off and last being seen billowing towards the Cyclades. Byron may have left his heart in Greece, Arthur left his hat.

If a fortnight at the cradle of civilisation failed to work its alchemy on Arthur's soul, it was a little more successful with his body. The first week's sunlight did nothing to his ghastly pallor except perhaps to cause some of the ginger freckles to cluster closer together for protection from the unaccustomed ultra-violet onslaught. But all at once his lard-like skin gave up the struggle and changed with all the suddenness of litmus paper dropped in pub wine.

He made the discovery when we were back in our new hotel room, drinking tea brewed in a toothglass and eating thin arrowroot biscuits – a civilising provision my mother had insisted upon including in our baggage. The loss of the hat had lowered Arthur's protective defences and his neck had become a bright pink. From that moment onwards Arthur seemed to have discovered his body. The prospect of being transfigured into a bronzed Adonis became a real possibility to him. By day he took to the beaches, and spent the night posing in front of the bedroom mirror in his underpants charting the progress of his tan with reference to the unspeakable paleness of his unexposed posterior. It was not a pretty sight, but it was an interesting one. Is this what happened to the ancient Greeks? I mused. It had taken them many centuries to move from culture-seeking idealists to sun-struck layabouts. Arthur had made the leap in seven days. Perhaps he'd suffered brain-damage as a result of all the noise at Glyfada. Whatever had happened, we had a much better time during the second week, when we stopped chasing around unfinished building sites and started lying in the sun and drinking cheap alcohol. And when Arthur, pink as a prawn, arrived back home at The Poet and Peasant, he was able to discourse learnedly about topless bathers and ouzo hangovers.

So much for the progress of civilisation.

SMITH INVADES THE CAPITAL

First broadcast February 1982

PEG RUGS AND PERSIAN CARPETS

A devout spiritualist once explained to me that a ghost was a poor confused and affrighted soul, which had been pitched out of this life so suddenly that it didn't know where it was; and would wander pale and disconsolate, until someone like himself came along and kindly showed it the doorway into the Great Yonder.

Now I know just the feeling. To step into an Intercity train and be bustled across the great divide between North and South in 2½ hours of lurching, point-rattling fury is every bit as bewildering and frightening to the living soul. Fortunately, to students of cultural warfare like myself there's no need of spiritual guidance: the moment I set foot on the train I began to read the signs of the impending gulf and prepared myself for the culture shock.

Fate found fit to place me in the same carriage as a figure who embodied all the light years of difference between Northern and Southern man and within minutes had me grinding my polystyrene tea-cup back into its constituent parts in dull rage. It was a posh accent, the superior Oxford drawl which D. H. Lawrence hated. But I didn't so much mind its superciliousness as its loudness. It was a two-carriages-plus-dining-car voice. Now we Northerners – as every Southerner knows – are generally apologetic: that's why we wear shawls and flat caps with buttons on the nebs which pull down, because we like to wander about unobtrusively. So to hear this voice drawling away without an ounce of self-consciousness seemed to belittle all our years of self-effacement. Like spending a lifetime whispering in church and then being told that God had never been there.

One girl spluttered with merriment into her embroidered handkerchief every time the restaurant car steward came on the tannoy. He was from Leeds, and it was the word 'breakfast' that prompted her derision. Well, it is break-fast, isn't it? It was break-fast for centuries, before you came along with your honed and manicured vowels, snapping off your consonants like twists of barley sugar.

Beyond Wakefield, as the allotments and striped pigeon huts start to thin out and the ragged armies of Brussels sprouts retreat in tattered disarray, a black man suddenly arrived in the seat opposite. He bore a vast cassette recorder at least a yard long. It comprised a baffling array of chrome buttons and knobs and glowing dials, more like a portable satellite tracking station. But no, a deft flick of a dozen switches and we had two hours of non-stop reggae music which by journey's end had me screaming out for the rhythmical sophistication of the old-fashioned railway track.

The journey is indeed a perfect acclimatisation to the absurdities of cosmopolitan life.

The Oxford voice was drawling on about the novels of Iris Murdoch. Miss Prim, who never takes break-fast, nibbled away at an apple like a canary at a caraway seed. A man opposite spent the entire journey reading the *Daily Express*, which must rank as one of the outstanding feats of human endurance in our time.

The train stops at Huntingdon. Now there's a vowel to snare the unwary Northern traveller. If he can pass that test, he's through the frontier and will pass unnoticed and untaunted into the stewpot of the metropolis. A crested grebe disappeared for ever under the ripples of a river as the train sped past. The earth, rich and dark, and darkly rumoured to be owned by Arabs, stretched to the flat sky, and we plunged down, coming to rest inside the great dome of King's Cross like rats in a cage.

'Do we know anybody?' whispers Arthur nervously. He's come with me, travelling free on what he calls his toothpaste ticket: an enlightened piece of modern marketing by British Rail, which entitles you to a month's free travel with any ticket-buyer if you send away enough toothpaste and soap-flake packets. You don't even have to think up a slogan, though I bet the regular travellers who have to pay through the nose can.

We retire to the station buffet to plan our assault on the capital and drink tea strong enough to make a Barnsley miner blanch. It sticks to the cup like molasses. Like travellers in search of Eldorado we decide to make for the West End. We pass a down-and-out meticulously foraging through the trash cans. He gives each bin his undivided attention, not wasting an ounce of energy on what other people might think.

On the underground Arthur is stabbed in the groin by an automatic ticket barrier then poked in the back with an umbrella for blocking the escalator. We emerge at Oxford Circus having shared the same air as seven million other human beings, or so it seems, and stand blinking in the alien daylight like Piltdown men. London roars over us like a flood tide. We decide to take refuge in a department store.

Now this turns out to be a mistake. Outside fairy stories where swineherds are changed into princelings, the human system cannot take in such sudden transformations. Three hours earlier we stood on Leeds station next to a fish train from Grimsby. Now we stand below a Tudor gallery festooned with Persian carpets and strewn with silks, our nostrils tickled by zephyrs of exclusive toiletries. Arthur, who furnishes his whole house from what he picks up at jumble sales, just wanders about crying, 'Cor, look how much this costs!' We reveal our true hillbilly vulgarity, I'm afraid, and the discreet and soft-soled floor-staff pad silently away to be out of earshot of our rude enthusiasm. But in our defence, I must say it's hard not to be overcome by the sight of a Persian carpet not much bigger than grannie's peg rug that costs £15,000.

'Who on earth can afford this sort of thing?' I gasp, trying the padlocks that secure them to the wall. As if on cue, the perfumed zephyr wafts the answer in a drawl of moneyed self-assurance: 'When one's fallen in love with something, one's never really satisfied with anything else.' The object of her amorous attention, a rug costing a cool £10,500, was being wheeled away by a youth with a porter's trolley. I'll bet the trash can man at the station would have given his right arm for a chance to rummage through *her* dustbin.

From the Aladdin's cave of the department store it's only a short culture-shocked stagger into the Eastern bazaar of Carnaby Street. A machine churns out clouds of bubbles into the reggae-loud air: a perfect image for Carnaby Street's flashy and tawdry transience: peacock colours swirling and dancing to every changing wind of modern fashion. There was a coven of girls with crazy fire-red hair, dyed and teased out to a listless frizz like nylon dusters. A youth passed by, his face tattooed to disfigurement; another bore a head shaven apart from a narrow, plastered plume, like an exotic cockatoo. Yet it gave him no pleasure. He strutted about muttering darkly like a dispossessed Mohican. In one shop which sold nose-bones and black plastic underwear, a black plastic girl, who shone like a well-oiled crow, picked over trinkets of silver, a beady shine to her corvine eye. She was surrounded by human skulls, the genuine article, ones that had once been filled with warm pulsing fluids and pulsing thoughts and feelings. What a place to come to rest, amongst the magpie baubles and trinkets of Carnaby Street, a sightless *memento mori* to all the heedless fripperies of youth.

Shops full of mirrors, of badges with slogans of pop and punk and plain tastelessness: 'Dead Kennedys' proclaimed one. Outside one shop a board is filled with thousands of badges, and I watch a youth stoop and winkle one out. Why that? What can it be? What slogan from so many can have captured his imagination? Some cosmic truth youth is privy to? I lean forward to glimpse the print, almost touching his shoulder in my eagerness. 'Shove off,' leers the message.

I suddenly wish I could, but I'm here for the week, to see if London really is the centre of the Universe. Carnaby Street obviously thinks it is. 'Carnaby Street Welcomes the World' shouts a sign draped across the whole street in typical Southern self-acclaim. Puff goes the bubble-machine and releases another shower of rainbow colours into the noisy air.

TERMITES AND OLD SCHOOL TIES

It strikes me that part of the secret of loving your fellow man comes from being able to keep him at a distance. That's why we're so friendly up here in the North where there's plenty of room to mind your own business: no shortage of windy moortops or decayed town centres where you can tramp about to your heart's content and never meet another soul. And when you do bump into somebody, look how pleasantly disposed it makes you for a cheery chat and a bit of friendly human intercourse.

But stick a chap on a London tube-train in the rush hour, half an inch from someone with hairs growing out of his ears and a passion for garlic sausage, and it's a bit harder to feel that same unalloyed joy at the proximity of one's fellows. After only one or two trips, limbs locked in a vice of congested bodies, forced, short of closing my eyes and feigning sleep, to inspect all the assorted blemishes of a sadly flawed humanity, I began to grow profoundly uncomfortable. The habitually happy grain of my disposition began to grow knotty and twisted. I found myself reading the tube notices: 'London Flooding is a Real Danger!' and longing for the sirens, the dull lap of the purging waters.

Today's journey, when we'd at last surfaced from the nightmare of the Underground, took us to the heart of the City. I've long had a yearning to visit the wondrous financial institutions of our ailing nation. Is there a human face, however blotched and moley, behind such mysterious measures of financial health as the FT Ordinary Share Index?

When you surface into the blinking daylight at Bank Station, you can tell at once you're there. The litter bins are stuffed with copies of the *Financial Times*. Buildings tall enough to keep the sun out all day. And cold. You'd have thought that with all that money about there'd be a feeling of warmth, of comfort about the City. But this was the cold engine-room of Empire, the lofty banks and exchanges, whose transactions powered the vaulting ambitions of cold-eyed, cold-hearted Victorian magnates. You think of the likes of Paul Dombey and shiver. And they're still there, the architects and financiers of these buildings, captured on the rooftops as they must have seen themselves in all their glorious megalomania, strutting round the stone friezes in the golden sunlight: naked gods and goddesses, heroes and conquerors.

But for my money, which is not a lot, the new National Westminster Tower beats all the pompous grandeur of the Victorians. It's like a main line to heaven, polished steel and glass to trap the sky and the sun, as flashy as anything in Dallas. Arthur, who has the soul of a socialist when it comes to such matters, said it looked like a giant silo, packed with fodder to stuff the gluttonous crops of the City slickers. And he points out the concrete wagon trundling away in the road underneath. 'Foundations are no good!' he announces.

Who was I to argue against such an observation on the precarious nature of our financial institutions?

Back on the streets, the messenger boys, proletarian versions of the City gents in dark suits shiny with wear, scuttle about like diligent beetles carrying their leather wallets. 'What's in them bags?' whispers Arthur, his eyes narrowing as he weighs up the prospect of a quick mugging and beating a hasty retreat to our fastness in the hills.

'It won't be cash,' I asserted. 'It's all bits of paper here. They don't have any money.'

I think Arthur had half-expected to see the champions of commerce behaving a bit like the local farmers at auction mart: spitting on their palms before they shook hands, then peeling off wads of notes from rolls as fat as a fist that lived deep down in a baggy trouser pocket.

We argued about this, until we decided to put it to the test. We'd walk into one of the buildings and ask to cash a cheque. It was hard deciding on which one, because they weren't all labelled. Those that were didn't sound too promising. The Bank of Nova Scotia looked very impressive, but Arthur insisted that they only dealt in furs and sealskins. We were too nervous to enter the Bank of Chicago, because of the man standing outside with the violin case. Eventually we decided upon an anonymous piece of portalled grandeur. Our progress across the daunting entrance lobby was halted by a pair of burly attendants in top hats and pink waistcoats.

'Where are we?' I asked, feeling a bit like Christopher Robin.

'The Bank of England, sir,' explained the splendid lackey with a slightly self-deprecating cough.

'Can I cash a cheque?' ventured Arthur.

He was clutching a well-creased passbook, which looked remarkably like one of those bank-books you used to take to junior school every Monday morning along with sixpence, or usually less if you'd bought some gobstoppers on the way.

'No, I'm afraid not, sir,' replied the doorman-cum-footman with a pitying smirk.

'No money?' I ventured in my turn with a gallant effort at humour. 'We'd heard things were bad.'

'There aren't many people have accounts here, sir,' explained the attendant.

Arthur was just launching into some preposterous nonsense about 'If this was supposed to be the Bank of England, English people should be able ...', when a party of gentlemen flanked by bodyguards in mohair suits and sunglasses, handcuffed to their briefcases, were ushered past us. We retired, with Arthur muttering darkly the sort of unenlightened views about our foreign cousins that no liberal-minded Radio 4 listener would care to hear repeated.

On the way to the Stock Exchange we passed a very discreet-looking tailor's, boasting that they were 'By Appointment to the Amir of Afghanistan'. It was full of old-school ties and sober pin-stripes, all the rage these days in the Khyber Pass, one must suppose.

After inspecting Arthur's World War II gas-mask bag for offensive weapons and finding only peanut butter sandwiches and a bottle of Newcastle Brown, the doormen allowed us into the public gallery of the Stock Exchange. It just looks like a giant termite mound with the lid off: full of urgent, yet to the uninitiated eye, strangely aimless seethings. Six or seven hundred men all dressed in the Amir of Afghanistan's suits, milling, gesticulating, hugger-muggering around the jobbers' hives. No visible queen to serve, no bloated rippling overblown bag of jelly to feed and spur on to lay more golden eggs. The metaphor, you may have guessed, was Arthur's, and I at once chastised him for it, pointing out that these were men of vision. See, the world was flashed up in lights before us; the minutes ticked away in San Francisco, Zurich, Johannesburg, Hong Kong. These were men of rare instinct who could sniff a quick buck across two continents. Through the glass of the gallery, muted but unmistakable came the buzz of hungry expectation. Something had aroused the age-old instinct of the pack-hunters and word was getting round: the hyenas had smelt the blood of the wounded wildebeest.

'These beggars closed our factory,' mumbled Arthur unreasonably.

'Nonsense, it was the unions,' I said, wanting to be on the right side in case someone heard and the pack rushed up the stairs.

'I wouldn't mind seeing a crash,' he went on.

Earlier we'd seen some men on the rooftop. 'Imagine them plunging down into Threadneedle Street,' went on Arthur gleefully. 'Pinstripes flapping in the wind like kamikaze jackdaws.'

I decided I'd better get him out and take him to Karl Marx's tomb at Highgate Cemetery.

As we left I reflected on how I'd not seen a pair of brown shoes or a smile all morning. The reason for the latter became apparent as we rode home on the tube. 'Shares Clobbered,' bawled the headlines of the *Standard*. This cheered Arthur up no end and he tried to strike up a friendly conversation with the lady next to him. She threatened to call the guard if he didn't stop molesting her. Civilised thing this Underground.

PARLIAMENT AND PORNOGRAPHY

It was at the age of thirteen, and I was at the threshold of that glandular catastrophe known as adolescence, which twenty-five to thirty years ago struck every young man and woman with all the guilty shame of indecent exposure. It hadn't quite hit me but I'd watched in mute dismay its effect upon an elder brother: the long hours locked alone in his room; the furtive rustle of secret literature; the ensuing pimples, unwanted hair; the hunted, haunted look when girls were mentioned. My grandfather, rather a stern figure, with a soaped moustache and a nose with pores like strawberry seeds, took me to one side. 'Boy,' he boomed, 'you are no longer a child.' At this I turned a violent pink colour, and my eyeballs began to sweat. 'You will soon be a man,' he went on, oblivious to my consternation. 'That means only one thing. You will start to take an interest ... in politics.'

Try as I would ever since, I'm afraid I've never been able to muster any genuine interest in the subject. So it was in a pious attempt to expiate the guilt I've always felt at this terrible failing that a visit to the House of Commons became a high priority on my sightseeing tour of the capital.

We decided to journey there by taxi, travelling in style down Park Lane, past Buckingham Palace and down the Royal Wedding route. But Arthur, who regularly takes his holidays at his auntie's in the People's Republic of South Yorkshire, spent the trip watching the taxi fare clocking up with all the hypnotic fascination of a rabbit watching a stoat.

The Palace of Westminster is awe-inspiring outside, especially at night with golden-yellow floodlights bathing the stonework. Arthur, who once had a job trimming flagstones with the Corporation, gawped in open-mouthed amazement at the south wall of the Abbey. Tracery as intricate as lace. We stood outside amongst the bustle of people coming in and out of the House. Clean-cut young identikit parliamentary private secretaries, thin-rimmed specs and worsted suits, whizz kids who have never failed to step sure-footed up every rung of the ladder from nursery school to Oxbridge and the Civil Service. Sparkling, finely milled cogs in the well-oiled machine of government. You feel you're at the top as well as at the centre of things here; a sort of heady self-importance comes over you simply by standing outside the House. Others must surely think of you like you think of them: that you're about some important affair of state. Mind you, when I saw Arthur fishing a can of pale ale out of his gas-mask bag, that thought perished.

Any self-importance you might feel starts to ebb when you enter Parliament; when you've been frisked and x-rayed at the door, eyed up and down by security police, and when you stand nervously under the vast chandelier in the central lobby and suddenly realise that you haven't the slightest idea of what your MP looks like, because you've only seen a fuzzy picture of him in your local paper opening a bring-and-buy sale.

Everybody seems to look like an MP in the central lobby, invested with an uncrumpled self-assurance. The exceptions are glaring. One poor chap looked like a latter-day Guy Fawkes, a bowed and brooding figure, nursing some private grievance like a boil. He's arguing with a young man at the desk, who's dressed in a morning coat and a white bow tie and who looks like an overgrown fag out of *Tom Brown's Schooldays*. He's very impressive until he starts to speak. Then he manages to sound like Liza Doolittle in her flower-selling days.

As we're led into the Public Gallery one of the doorkeepers demands to know if I'm a sex-shop proprietor. I don't quite know how to deal with this one and feel very confused, as though Grandfather was back again interrogating me. Only when we enter the Chamber and I hear a reference to 'instruments inflicting sexual cruelty and violence' and look at the order paper, do I realise that they're debating a bill to license sex-shops. I settle down with growing curiosity.

From what you hear on radio you get the impression that the Chamber is always like a rugby club stag night with the Speaker vainly trying to keep order like a licensee desperate to preserve the good name of his establishment. It's not at all like that. These are the edited highlights, the action replays of exciting goalmouth rucks and mêlées. There are long periods of soporific inaction in between, when the ball is lost and half the players have wandered off for tea. We sat through such a period. You'd have thought a subject as emotive as sex would have aroused some passion. Not a bit of it. It was all as exciting as the reproductive cycle of the earthworm. And the trouble is, once you're in the Public Gallery, it's difficult to get out without causing a major disturbance, the seats are packed so tight together.

However, I managed to devise a game to relieve some of the tedium. It involved awarding points to Government or Opposition according to various observable foibles and idiosyncrasies. The scoring went something like this: Leg up over bench in front: Government 1, Opposition 1. Lying on bench: Government 0, Opposition 2. Wearing sports jackets: Government 0, Opposition 4. Talking during debate: Government 15, Opposition 15. Snoring: see House of Lords score sheet. Sleeping: Government 5, Opposition 5. It was while I was thus engaged in this innocent means of staying awake myself that I received a poke from one of the attendants. Did I know that I was not permitted to write in the Chamber? If I continued, I would incur the wrath of the Speaker.

Things did liven up a bit after that. Someone got up and began to denounce sex-shops as poisonous fungi springing up in our society. Everyone else seemed to spring up at that point. There was even some laughter as we rode briefly upon the indignant member's flight of rhetoric. But it wasn't long before he sat down and the Waters of Lethe lapped over us again. Fortunately, Arthur, who has his uses, shortly after that became stricken with cramp and had to be carried out of the Chamber to much hissing and waving of order papers.

In a desperate bid to enliven our leaden spirits we made for Soho. I was anxious to know in just what way I resembled a sex-shop proprietor. True, I did have dreadful bags under my eyes, but this was because our hotel bedroom was next to a main road and I hadn't slept a wink since we arrived in London.

We called first at a quiet pub which seemed to sit quite comfortably amongst the love shops whose seductively swaying bead curtains separated us from what was described as 'a garden of erotic delights'. We'd decided to forego the amusements of a topless bar further down the street because Arthur was afraid he'd have nowhere to rest his drink. In the very normal pub we were joined by an ultra-normal-looking party of three women and a man. He could have been a junior cabinet minister, and the women looked as though they'd taken a wrong turning on their way to the AGM of the Women's Institute.

'What will you have to drink?' asked the man.

'Oh, ah, ah!' stammered the first woman as though fending off the naughtiest suggestion of her life.

What on earth were they doing here next to the Spanking Cinemas and Cupid's Bookshops? Less inscrutable, for a change, was the party of immaculately dressed diminutive Japanese businessmen clucking appreciatively as they emerged from an ill-lit basement.

I finally got my wish and saw a sex-shop proprietor. He was standing in the doorway of a cinema whose moving neon display announced: 'Desire and Perversion, Two hours of best adult film now showing. OAPs £2.' Trade was poor, not a single walking-frame in the foyer, and he looked very downcast. For a minute I thought it might have been the Guy Fawkes we saw in the central lobby of the House.

As we turned away we glimpsed the moon climbing over the rooftops of Greek Street. 'Looks like frost,' said Arthur without much passion. 'Shall we go home?'

If I'd been asked to vote on the motion: Which had

turned out to be more lively – the Chamber of the House or Soho, sex or politics?, I'd have been hard pressed to know which way to vote. Either way, I think the yawns would have it.

ODOURS OF THE ABYSS

When I first came down to London as a student, reluctantly released from the bosom of a tearful mum, with a travelling trunk stuffed full of home-made fruit cakes and woolly vests, I was ill-prepared for the spartan standards of the South. Through even the grimmest post-war days, as kids we'd ploughed our way through corner cuts of beef and steamed puddings. We were round and pink and full of goodness as Christmas turkeys. Meanwhile, alas, Mum skimped and scavenged and did without for us like an anxious mother hen. So you can imagine my dismay, when I arrived that first day at my London digs, to be faced with a plate of tuna paste sandwiches and a thin slice of Battenburg cake left curling under a tea-towel. And that was supposed to be Sunday lunch!

Had I chanced upon a pocket of poverty and underprivilege left over from the days of Dickens here in the heart of the uncaring city? Not a bit of it. When I eventually caught up with my gadfly landlady, I met with a vision of splendour more in keeping with the Royal Enclosure at Ascot than Acton Town. Festooned with jewels and furs and plastered with exclusive cosmetics, she was a walking advert for Bond Street.

Now, we have a none too elegant but very apt phrase for this in the North of England, and it was the one Arthur came up with to describe London after three days there: 'All fur coat and no knickers.'

Take our hotel. The reception area was plush and inviting, the lounge and dining room posh enough to start Arthur whispering and sounding his h's. But journey upstairs from one landing to the next, and the veneer of civilisation fell away before your eyes. By the time we reached our room, all pretensions to refinement and comfort had disappeared. The fur coat was off (back in the hands of the hire purchase company), and what we were really expected to put up with for our £20 a night was exposed in all its shameful nakedness. It was little more than a garret, a shabby affair with patched and peeling walls. There was a stained sink with pipes that grumbled and muttered all night long and an assortment of furnishings that would have disgraced Her Majesty's Prison Service. But the crowning glory was the view from the window. A peek-a-boo behind the handsome facade of our fabled city. Rank gardens choked with rubbish; all the detritus of life piled against the back door. It was a good job the window didn't open, because from it all arose the unmistakable odour of the abyss.

Arthur, whose mum still donkey-stones her back step and disinfects her dustbin once a week, slumped onto the bed in a sudden fit of depression. 'Never mind,' I said, drawing the curtains. 'You can watch telly.'

This was one of the hotel's luxuries, which in the newspaper ad had persuaded us we were going to spend the week in style. It had turned out to be a yellowing plastic thing with a picture which rolled over and over like a floundering fish until you took your fist to it. But Arthur wasn't going to be consoled by any cheap technological gimmicks. He was sure his dad had forgotten to feed his pigeons and that his whippets were pining away for him. He grew horribly homesick. After a terrible night spent tossing and turning to a ceaseless cacophony of pipes and firedoors, traffic, drunks, and low-flying aircraft, Arthur surfaced next day like a claustrophobic mole. London had got squarely on top of him. Seven million people had sat on him all night, breathed his air, generally fouled his living space, and come between him and that daily quota of privacy and peace which prevents us all from degenerating into mad axemen or reservoir poisoners.

Arthur had got to be got out of London for a while.

I grabbed the map and searched desperately for some green bits. London squatted there like a fat toad, its black haunches stretching miles into the surrounding shires. Arthur would never last as far as Box Hill. Then a sudden inspiration. If I took him up the Post Office Tower, that would help him to recover his sense of perspective, restore the innate superiority of the proud Northern hill-dweller over his crawling Southern counterpart.

We emerged from the great lavatory that is Tottenham Court Road tube station. In the subway I had to drag Arthur away from the mournful strains of an exiled folk singer, who had him keening in unison like a destitute dachshund.

Tottenham Court Road seems to have become the stainless steel shrine of the new video age, shop upon shop of new-fangled gadgetry, playthings for an ostrich generation to sit and gawp at, and fiddle away with the knobs as the world burns. I've never seen so many people clutching hi-fi equipment with earphones clamped upon their empty heads to keep them from lolling off.

Of course, as everybody knows apart from us bumpkins, the Post Office Tower was closed, out-of-order like a vandalised phone box. I wasn't surprised. I'd tried 13 times to get a connection in a phone box earlier that day. London phones seem to be as chancy as computer dating. Arthur didn't believe that terrorists had closed the tower, but thought it was to deter suicide. He was getting worse, and struck up a morbid conversation with a down-and-out, who struggled along like a dung beetle under three overcoats, five carrier-bags, and a long brush. What was the long brush for? Arthur said he was the Grim Sweeper.

I whisked him down into the Underground and headed for the Northern Line. Just the word bucked him up. We sat in the same compartment as a man who kept humming to himself and waving his arms about. Arthur was sure he was a loony and wanted to move to another seat. But I pointed out that he was probably a composer or a conductor practising his arm movements. After all, this was London where they did have that sort of thing.

We got off at a place called Kilburn. The name had something of a rustic ring to it and we thought we might find some open spaces; perhaps the odd sylvan glade, where swains cavorted in russet mantle clad.

We picked our way through the scrummage of second-hand shops, Asian fruiterers, and Irish newsagents: 'Place your order for the *Limerick Leader*.' Past all the display cards: 'Double rooms to let, suit boys only.' 'Attractive model seeks unusual position.' All before us stretched the grey horizon of bed-sit land: huge neglected houses flanked by scrofulous plane trees and rusting motorcars.

We scuttled back to take refuge in a tea-shop and I engaged two of the local tribeswomen in conversation. 'How do you get out into the country?' I enquired.

'Eow,' said the first, greeting the question with the sort of startled puzzlement you'd expect if I'd asked her for a blood transfusion. 'Yeow want the M1. Doesn't he, Doris?'

'Hemel Hempstead,' volunteered Doris. 'That's where the country is. Hemel Hempstead.'

The tube didn't go as far as Hemel Hempstead so we got off at Pinner. No unpleasant odours here. We'd left behind the slattern anonymity of the city. Here you could see the middle-class pressure to keep the Joneses toeing the line in every pruned rosebush and painted flower tub. There was a twee high street with a flush of antique shops and Tudor tea-rooms as prim as a bunch of sweet peas. There was a half-price sale of gold-plated taps in the kitchen shop. And a bottle bank, where in Kilburn they make do with the gutter. The only second-hand shop in Pinner was Dr Barnardo's. It had all the cosiness of well-shod, well-groomed suburbia. Here, women walked into the hairdressers who looked as though they'd just come from the hairdressers.

'I'm going over to Marjorie's at Haslemere,' announced a voice, its owner clad in full-length silver-fox fur.

Arthur and I stopped dead in our tracks. It was the voice. The same smug drawl which had wafted in and out of our lives these past three days South of Watford. We'd run it down to its source. Its message was quite clear. We were here at the centre of the Universe. We need look no further for human perfection.

I looked at Arthur. The colour was back in his cheeks and his eyes burnt with the old fire.

'Back to the abyss?' I suggested.

'You bet,' he replied.

LIVE SHOWS AND DEAD BEER

One of the arguments people use for not doing the sensible thing and turning their backs on London for ever is that it's the cultural mecca of our island. That to tramp the mountains of Wales, loiter in the Dales of North Yorkshire, or wiggle your toes in the rock pools of Galloway may be all right for a week or ten days in the summer. But to live there would be tantamount to spiritual and intellectual self-mutilation. The total man can never be fulfilled unless he lives in or within easy access of London, whose theatres and concert halls, restaurants and wine-bars are nothing less than a Parnassian spring of inspiration and delight at which all truly civilised people must sip deep and tremble with ecstasy.

The corollary of this deep-rooted and widespread myth is that beyond the sublime cultural halo, which encircles London, particularly northwards, all is darkness and outer night, an arid region peopled by stunted primitives with souls of fishmongers.

Now, hailing from a town whose nearest thing to the theatre of the absurd is its local council chamber, and where eating out generally refers to fish and chips in the street, who were Arthur and I to question the truth of the myth? We approached the West End with all the piety of pilgrims about to kiss holy relics. Of course, the trouble is that the pathway to culture, like good taste, is never well signposted. If that were the case, it would become too well-beaten a highway, and there'd be no distinction in getting there if, when you arrived, you found the unwashed mob had already set up camp. So the big question was, which show should we take in?

'Great art is that which hath withstood the test of time,' declaimed Arthur with much solemnity. So we bought two tickets to *No Sex Please, We're British!* because, according to the blurb, it's now in its '11th hysterical year'.

But before sating the spirit on the ambrosia of art, we had to attend to the needs of the body. So we popped into a rather trendy little wine-bar. It was as bustling with theatre folk as a foyer at a world premiere. Not that we recognised any stars, just the odd vaguely familiar face: now was she in the last television Shakespeare, or is she the girl in the dandruff ad? It was all very exhilarating, brushing shoulders with the nearly famous in the heady wine-dark atmosphere of Nos Caves Piccadilly.

Regrettably, London is no different from Crewe or

Bingley, if you're a stranger to the place. All signs and notices are written for people who know already. Everybody else had got their food and drink, while we stood gaping uncomprehendingly at all the chalked noticeboards as if they were the Dead Sea Scrolls. The main difficulty was that all the wine seemed to be sold by the bottle, and we only wanted the odd glass. I didn't want any trouble from Arthur. He was already starting to get disruptive.

'Order a bin end,' he advised, 'then we'll have something to sit on. Ha!'

There is something, alas, about the Northern temperament that, when faced with what it sees as over-refinement, reverts to a sort of primitivism. Arthur's answer to all the posturing young wine connoisseurs was to retreat to this twilight zone like a threatened animal that backs to the mouth of its cave and starts to growl and make faces. With a glass of house red inside him, things didn't improve. The sight of a Greek menu which consisted of what Arthur construed to be humus and crudities had him pointing and cackling like a Bedlamite. The bright young Thespians and their followers shrank back in distaste as if they'd found a spider in the Margaux. Blessedly a table became vacant from which we were less conspicuous and I had the opportunity to look round.

We were next to a stringy creature with sharp features and staring eyes who pecked away at a dish of olives like a fastidious blue-tit. She was trying to impress her friend with a display of one-upmanship that made Fanny Craddock seem self-effacing. She was moving into a flat, while Jeremy went to Japan to collect antiques and Celia popped off to New York to study interior design. The pied-à-terre was divine with bidets on the patio and jacuzzis on the mezzanine.

She went on and on like a house agent while her friend parried the overwhelming barrage of status symbols with the dead inscrutability of a natterjack toad. I sank my teeth into a French loaf and left them there to save grinding them to dust, while Arthur lifted up a dish of cranberry sauce and enquired loudly what the jam was for.

Over in the corner a most unpromising-featured young man whose hairline had begun to recede in search of his missing chin was darting hungry glances at a dazzling young actress. He looked to have about as much chance of success as a vineyard in Hartlepool. But how wrong can you be? Ten minutes and a few more swigs of the warm South and he'd chatted her up. For the young, London really is a city of dreams, dreams that can come true!

The wine had worked for us too. Two glasses had released our cultural inhibitions and we were ready for a good laugh. 'Hysterically funny. Makes one proud of the theatre,' announced the critic of one newspaper. 'Yells of laughter, seizures of mirth!' proclaimed the other.

Now far be it from me, a mere hillbilly, to impugn the reputations of these illustrious journals by naming them, but I'd advise them to keep a tighter rein on the expense accounts of their theatre critics in future, for I can only conclude that whoever wrote that must have been drunk, so drunk as to be totally insensible to the puerile nonsense that passed for theatrical comedy. The only yells I let out were ones of anguish; the only seizures, those of my mind grinding to a standstill in paralysed dismay. If the springs of Parnassus run with this sort of stuff, I'd rather be back amongst the North Country Calibans sipping the green mantle off stagnant ponds out of an old Wellington boot.

In fairness to all concerned, however, I must say that by no means everybody felt this way. We were surrounded by a giggling, guffawing mob, so much so that at one stage I decided that we'd not come to the West End at all, but had been mysteriously transported to Mars and dropped amongst an alien race.

Tongues and minds furred like old pipes with the wine and 'entertainment' of the evening, we decided that a glass of wholesome ale might cleanse and restore us. After all, this was the London of Samuel Johnson, of Dylan Thomas, whose alehouses overflow with the wit and wisdom of vintage conversation. We hurried to a pub, thirsty of soul and body.

We opened the door to be hit by an avalanche of decibels. A rock concert, amplified to mayhem, was in full swing on a huge screen at the far end of the bar. It was flanked by four television sets all showing rival attractions. Opposite were ranged the loudspeakers, pounding their deafening roar into the smoke-filled air. We lurched for the bar like troops coming over the top. It was a comprehensive assault on all the senses. Even the beer smote the palate like liver salts, dead of all taste and flavour. Fizz of no substance or value, like the video Babel around us. The pictures were a garble of crazily juxtaposed images. On the big screen the entire workforce of a Japanese zip factory was jiving to Siouxsie and the Banshees. Next door a camera lingered over a medieval painting, a study in pious suffering. On another screen doctors performed an operation, dipping inside a patient and pulling out strings of glistening things. On the fourth screen, amongst all the uproar a newsreader struggled manfully with *News at Ten*.

'Bloody hell!' gasped Arthur.

It was hell, pure hell. And it was full. Full of shades, lost souls, young men and women clad in black leather, drinking the Lethean waters and raising their fists to the graven images on the screen in time to the hideous din.

I tried to drag Arthur away but his eyes were suddenly glued to one of the television sets. It was the football results.

'Burnley's won!' he yelled joyously. 'Let's have another drink.'

I groaned. What do you expect from a Northerner? All beer and football. Now what we need is a bit of culture, like they've got in the South.

I'D RATHER BE LOCKED IN THE TOWER

It was our last day and Arthur announced at breakfast that he just wanted to be an ordinary tourist. Forget about all this amateur sociology and North versus South stuff, let's just enjoy some of the sights before we go home. As he spoke he slid slices of toast into his pocket. 'For the pigeons in Trafalgar Square,' he whispered.

Our whole approach had been wrong up till now, he went on, to regard London as a place, where normal people lived and worked. It must be viewed like Stonehenge or Blackpool Zoo, as a spectacle to be marvelled over, pointed at, and, of course, fed with slices of toast.

But old habits die hard, and as Arthur cooed and clucked at the pigeons on the steps below Nelson's Column, and the birds fluttered and jostled for his toast in their grey thousands, I couldn't help thinking that the trouble with London was its scale. It had become unmanageable, like a fat stomach. Someone should have called a halt a long time ago, before it put the island off balance, throwing all the weight and influence to one end and creating all the trouble and resentment in Darwen and Motherwell and the like. Now a rival centre of government in Hebden Bridge would really set the see-saw swinging!

Whitehall is coldly overawing. Plain, grey stonework, the huge black doors of the offices. It's the cold, impassive facade of the administration: the Civil Service. Not a bit like the extravagant and ornate stonework further down the road at Westminster, which fits the passion and absurdity of politics.

We had hoped to get a glimpse of our redoubtable Leader at Downing Street. But No 10 was closed – a suspicion we've all had in the North long before unemployment reached three million. There were gates across the street and a policeman on duty.

'Can we just have a look in? We've come a long way,' wheedled Arthur after asking for his autograph. The policeman told him to move on, but let a little old lady with a shopping bag through.

'There she goes!' shouted Arthur and caused a minor sensation amongst a coachload of German tourists.

'Zat is your Premier?' cried one incredulous Hun.

'Aye,' replied Arthur, who doesn't like Germans after spending a week in a hotel full of them at Marbella, 'she's just been round the corner to t' Co-op for a loaf and two eggs.'

I dragged him away before there was another war. It was just after eleven, and they were changing the guard at Horse Guards Parade. Two rows of mounted cavalry faced each other. The men all looked like Oliver Reed, and the horses champed and rolled their pink-grey tongues round their bits like old men with peanuts down their dentures. I marvelled at the restraint of the men outside with their swords. People kept coming up and patting their horses and feeding them chocolate. I'd have had their fingers off with that sword in the time it takes to cry 'Balaclava!'

My thoughts grew even more bloodily disposed when we arrived at Tower Hill. Arthur went scampering around looking for a scaffold and bloodstains on the grass in Trinity Gardens. I sat on a bench near a bronze statue of a Roman emperor with his finger in the air looking as though he was feeding the pigeons.

'Now there was a woman for you,' I observed ruminatively. 'Boadicea. Burned the whole place down and murdered everybody. 60 AD. Things weren't much different in those days from what they are now,' I went on, looking over towards the new skyscrapers of the City, choking the ancient foundations: Aldgate, Houndsditch, St Mary Axe, St Botolph's, the Ward of Portsoken. 'They may have been Roman imperialists then, but they had the same idea, to get rich by exploiting the natives, the provincials.'

'So she came along and burned it all down?' whispered Arthur, suddenly interested. A murderous gleam had entered his eye and I could see he was thinking of getting a few of the lads together when he got back home. But any enthusiasm for insurrection soon cooled when we arrived at the Tower and leaned over the moat at Traitor's Gate. Even today, with the sunlight scattered on the Thames it looked cold and dank, a one-way hopeless gateway to the block.

Inside we were met by a Beefeater, built like a Welsh scrum-half. I can't see why Beefeaters are regarded with so much affection. The one we got involved with was terrifying. We were wandering casually towards the Bloody Tower when he rounded us up like a snappy terrier and made us join his conducted tour. He had a great round voice like a tun of ale and a way of looking everybody in the eye at once so you didn't dare not pay attention. I didn't like this a bit. I hadn't paid £2 to be bullied. Mind you, he was very good, reciting his catalogue of murder, duplicity and malice. It made the Borgias sound like Quakers compared to the kings of England.

The Jewel House was closed – I think they'd heard that Arthur was coming – but it didn't seem to matter, because the real gems of the Tower are black, rowdy, and bad-tempered. Outside the White Tower the ravens lolloped about the lawns screeching abusively at passers-by, litter-bins, and creation in general. Our sergeant-major Beefeater had just raked us all into an attentive line with his menacing eye, when Arthur, observing one bird jabbing spitefully at an empty paper bag, tossed it a slice of toast. The sergeant major glared balefully, but went on with his monologue, a tale of horrid executions before crowds of eager onlookers. The raven attacked Arthur's toast so violently that it speared it on its bill, right up over the bridge, until it covered its face. The bird let out an enraged caw and began staggering and flapping about like a nun in a hurricane. A hundred pairs of eyes slid cautiously away from the Beefeater to watch this extraordinary spectacle.

'And before the blood had dried on the block–' boomed the Beefeater, eyes blazing at Arthur.

'Haw, haw, haw,' screeched the blindfolded raven lurching into a litter-bin, where it contrived to peel off the impaled toast. The Beefeater, realising that he was being upstaged, along with 500 years of English history, turned on the bird and shooed it away, whence it departed hooting and cackling like a witch.

I decided it would be prudent to leave before we were incarcerated. Not that I'd have minded. The Tower struck me as being an ideal place to live in London, with a moat and fifteen-feet-thick walls to keep everybody else at bay. Certainly the Bloody Tower looked a darn sight more comfortable than our hotel had been.

With a couple of hours still to spare before our train we dashed across London to the Natural History Museum. Arthur had a date with a dinosaur which he'd been promising himself all week. The dinosaur had been waiting a bit longer. We sat on a seat about halfway along 30 yards of articulated bone and grappled with perspective. But our minds were swimming long before we'd reached the 70 million years of the Upper Cretaceous period. Arthur put his fist in an eye-socket and got a scowl from an attendant. There was something wrong. Our imaginations had failed to stir. Tired? No. The realisation came suddenly. It was all dead. London is many things, and I've said quite a few nasty things about it, but you can't accuse it of being dead, and after a week we weren't prepared for this comprehensive lifelessness. We'd have given a case full of stuffed coelacanths for just one mean glint of a raven's eye.

We mooched about disconsolately amongst the bones. 'Pterodactyls don't appear to have teeth after all,' I observed. Arthur said he'd known all along because he'd paid particular attention to Raquel Welch's body when she was dropped from the beak of one in the film *One Million Years BC*. There hadn't been a scratch.

He wandered off to stare at a stuffed angler fish. It looked like a death's head with a bright lure to catch its victim.

'I wonder what's for tea when we get back,' I heard him mutter.

We just caught the train before it shot us out of London like a cork from an airgun. Like our arrival, our departure didn't make the slightest ripple in the great ocean of humanity we'd left behind. I think we both felt small, as if we'd been still sitting there next to the dinosaur. Anyway, neither of us spoke until after Watford, and then it didn't seem to matter so much and we both began to breathe more easily.

SMITH ON SURVIVAL

First broadcast May 1980

BALE MONEY

Do you ever have one of those ghastly dreams where you're trying to catch a bus, but however hard you run you just can't make it? They say it's a sign of frustration. If this is true, my frustration is enough to make Ixion's wheel sound like something on a funfair. You see, in my dreams, I not only never catch the bus, which is supposed to be whisking me away from somewhere I hate profoundly – usually London – but I never get anywhere at all. I just go round and round in circles. And, if this wasn't enough, a new thread has recently become tangled up in the ravelled knot of my subconscious. My escape now involves passage across some tract of water. Yes, you've guessed it. The bank from which I've fled never recedes, and the shore of my destination never gets any nearer. Moreover, the boat has sprung a leak, and however furiously I bale, the water continues to rise.

The sad truth is, I'm sinking fast. My brain has only just caught up with the desperate nightly messages my stricken subconsious has been flashing. For years I've been floating along comfortably in an economic limbo, oblivious of the fact that I was getting nowhere; lulled by my own gentle baling action. The trouble is I'd failed to notice the hole in the boat had been getting bigger and the water-level has now reached my chin.

My first instinct when faced with financial ruination is to borrow. Now I know that this course of action will meet with very little approval from many of you. It's the typical reaction of a spineless generation of grab-it-while-you-can hedonists. It's just the sort of behaviour that got us into this boat in the first place. My parents' generation would gladly don sackcloth, put the dishcloth on to boil, send back the crystal set and sit and sing hymns round an empty grate. But theirs is a generation that still feels guilty about luxury. 'Suffering is good for you' was a precept learnt on grandma's knee. To unabashed sybarites of the promise-crammed '50s and '60s, for whom every cockleshell held a pearl and every molehill afforded a prospect of lands of plenty, self-sacrifice doesn't come at all easily.

So, borrow. A larger bucket to bale myself out. Casually running my eye along the half-yearly profits of my bank and losing count of the number of noughts, I decide on a quick search of the wardrobe to see if my friendly local bank manager is thereabouts. I have to report that this creature is now extinct as a domestic species. He has been replaced by credit cards and cash dispensers with withdrawal ceilings of Shylockian stinginess. He who would see him now must fight his way into the vaults, where he lies curled up amongst the safe-deposit boxes, a digital display unit fixed to the top of his head, a thin trail of ticker-tape dribbling from his lips.

The wardrobe contains my only suit – weddings, funerals, and interviews, though it's not been used for the latter purpose ever since it became known that I've worked for the BBC. There's a fine dusting of mildew on the lapels. As I remove the suit a moth drops out, belly like a ripe catkin, surfeited with worsted. I think of how nature exploits every opportunity, how one creature's misfortune is another's improvement. The thought somehow brings me back to the bank. I ring for an appointment.

I enter the panelled office and it feels like school again. 'Well, Smith, capsized the school eight, eh?' I expect to see him flexing a cane beneath the desk. But he's not, he's hiding a carton of fig rolls. He's not the grey-jowled, leather-bound cash-ledger I'd expected. His cheeks are pink as the pages of the *Financial Times*, and he wears a suit like Rupert Bear's father. I'm deeply suspicious. They're getting damned clever with these robots these days. 'G-o-o-d m-o-r-n-i-n-g,' I feel like saying to try to catch him out. But there's no need. He speaks perfectly normally and offers a warm hand with just a hint of stickiness about one finger – the one where they wear the little rubber porcupine thing to count out the banknotes. I'm encouraged.

'Now, how can we help you?' he asks.

'Well, it's a question of staying afloat. I have this cash

flow problem.' To impress him I've mastered some of his jargon by reading through the index of H. Hughes *Banking Can Be Fun.* 'It seems to be flowing away from me faster than it arrives,' I add, immediately destroying any impression of an orderly, creditworthy mind. By now it's awash with maritime imagery. I even have to restrain myself from making a Canute-like gesture and pushing against his desk with my outstretched arms.

He smiles at his blotter. Then I notice that he's got in front of him an account statement with my name on top.

This is probably not the time to ask him what the initials DR after the last entry mean. There used to be a girl called Doris Redman worked behind the counter, but that was years ago, before I sprang the leak. I suppose they could have her hidden away in the accounts department.

'How much would you be needing?' he asks.

This is more like it. I reach for the bucket with both hands.

'Oh, say a thousand.'

It's only now that I begin to realise that there's something profoundly furtive about Mr Bear. He's not looked directly at me once. I'm sure it's not the fig rolls, though I think it's mean of him not to offer me one. Perhaps he's waiting until we've got business over.

The note-counting finger suddenly takes on a life of its own and begins dancing ecstatically up and down on the buttons of his pocket calculator.

'A £1000 personal loan over a year at 22 per cent will mean monthly repayments of £101.67 pence.' He smiles. I can hear the edges of his mouth creaking.

For the first time he looks up and I see his eyes. I have looked into the eyes of a goat and been amazed to find a creature with rectangular pupils. Mr Bear's pupils are shaped like pound signs and the curve at the top bears a wicked spike like a fish-hook.

'Er, yes. Er, oh!' I flounder. 'There's just one snag. I won't be able to pay anything back for, er – six months?'

The pound signs disappear, whirring round like the windows in a one-armed bandit until they become a blur, a frosty glaze.

'I beg your pardon?'

I rise on the gathering surf, unsteadily, but gradually gaining momentum.

'This idea. I've got this wonderful idea for a book. Only it will take me a few months to write it, and then there'll be publishing delays. So ideally, I'd like a year. Yes, a year before it gets into the best-selling charts.'

'Idea?'

I am losing him. The eyes have dropped back to the blotter and I can hear the crinkling of the fig rolls wrapper. I try desperately to fire the imagination of this desiccated cheque-processor.

'Yes. It's about this giant moth pupa that lies buried underneath Silbury Hill. It's lain hidden there for centuries, from a past age when insects were vast, like reptiles once were, and like banks are now. And, anyhow, changes in the earth's climate bring it out and it starts to wreak havoc, gobbling everything else up. And it's able to communicate with other pupae buried under the network of neolithic monuments throughout the world, and civilisation as we know it is threatened! Until this scientist hits on the idea of – drowning them.'

My flimsy surf-board has flipped and I am plunging headlong into the depths.

Mr Bear has risen, stowing the fig rolls firmly away in his desk drawer as if they are his private collection of

Krugerrands; he is showing me the door.

'Herman Melville had to live while he wrote *Moby Dick*,' I cry from the threshold, causing as much commotion at the counter as the abolition of interest charges. 'Look at the loss to civilisation if he'd have starved to death. I suppose you'd have lent me it if I'd wanted to open a fish-and-chip shop. Where are your priorities?'

I am suddenly breasted by two security men in helmets and chinstraps and frogmarched out with all the decorum they usually reserve for bag-loads of copper.

That night I dreamt someone did lend me a bucket for £220. But when I started to bale with it, it didn't seem to do much good. There was no bottom in it.

A LILY RECONSIDERED

Biblical sayings are like wet soap. Just when you think you've got a firm grip on them they go squirting off through your fingers and disappear into some unfathomed region of the bathtub.

'Consider the lilies of the field, they toil not neither do they spin.'

For a long time I was a lily of the field: my hands waxsmooth, my mind uncorrupted by any vile notions of gain. We did our own thing in those days, like they said we could, in the decade of the duffer, when every day was a prize day and no one came last. I wrote an epic poem about the disease of materialism called 'Jerusalem in Chains', and associated with people who distinguished themselves by creating sculptures out of bed-springs and making seed collages.

But lilies wither. I got fed up of sharing a clapped-out Ford Popular with the petrol-gauge always empty when I came to drive it, tired of hunting for needles of animal protein in haystacks of rice. I began to derive a certain spiritual comfort from settling down after a good steak supper amongst my few modest possessions and reading through the swelling entries in my building society pass book.

'Lay not treasures up on earth, where moth and rust doth corrupt.'

Now here's more subversive stuff, sticking a spanner in the spokes of honest capitalism. In our town it would set them fidgeting for their antacid tablets at the Rotary Club luncheon, and in the tap room of The Thieving Magpie spluttering with mirth into their brown ale. You see, if hoarding is a measure of human corruption, then I live in Gomorrah. Here, hoarding is a tribal religion. But it's worth more than a passing glance as the flood-waters of financial ruination begin to rise.

Take Ellis Lonsdale's shed: a ramshackle hotch-potched affair of packing cases and tarpaulin, which looks like a cross between a refugee camp and a rest home for grounded racing pigeons. In fact, it's an ark. Inside you'll find two of everything – and he's had most of them for so long they've multiplied. He could fit out the Ragged School, repaint the Post Office Tower – though it would probably end up looking like a barber's pole – and refit a DC10. How Ellis stocks his ark is one of twilight's mysteries. His second-hand breadvan glides noiseless as a hearse from one bankrupt business to the next. Ten minutes before a jumble sale begins, a figure remarkably like his slips out of the back door with a sack on his back. He has a deeply sympathetic nature, too. When death empties a house, he's there before the undertaker, passing on his respects while making a bid for the furniture.

Transactions at Ellis's take place with all the circumspection of a masonic handshake. Men, macs tied up with string, stand about casually aiming swings at clods of mud with their Wellington boots, gazing pensively into the middle distance, eyes never meeting until bargains are struck and palms meet in a rustle of banknotes. But these are Ellis's equals. They know so much about screwing one another down they should have been bookbinders. When I went recently to get hold of some stone for a fireplace, he spent so long rubbing his horny hands together I thought he was trying to strike sparks. Yes, he had just the thing, best quality sandstone, cut and dressed. If I'd like to call back in half an hour. When I returned, there they were, looking very ordinary and not too clean – I was sure that was a lump of moss he'd just kicked off one of the stones. He picked up another and pressed it to his ear. Did I know this one had come out of an old Methodist chapel? If you listened carefully you could still hear the echo of the organ. A piece of history, and a bargain at six quid a yard. I bought two yards. It was not long afterwards that a friend pointed out that a gap of about the same length had recently appeared in the wall behind Ellis's ark.

Ellis will still be afloat when I'm turned to fish paste, and when he dies such wealth will come to light as will make Captain Flint's treasure look like a waiter's tip at a Burns' Night dinner.

By now you may have guessed why I'm telling you all this. After last week's failure to persuade the bank manager to invest in me, I decided the only other way to postpone the evil hour, when cuts would have to be made in my comfortable life-style, was to realise some of my assets.

I had reluctantly decided to sacrifice one of my treasured possessions: an astronomical telescope, an instrument that had afforded me hours of diversion from my sublunary cares. That is, until recently, when I had to stop using it.

Certain vile rumours were put about that I had it trained upon the bedroom window of the lovely Mavis Tattersall. I swear this is untrue. I have no idea which house she lives in in Zeebrugge Terrace – besides, they always keep the curtains drawn there.

Anyhow, having decided to part with the instrument, I advertised my intention in the weekly edition of the *Gomorrah Gleaner*. On the eve of publication there came a knock on my door. It was Ellis Lonsdale.

'I've come about yon microscope,' he announced.

'Telescope,' I corrected.

'Aye, that's it,' he grunted, elbowing his way past.

I was on the point of closing the door when something shot out of the shadows and followed him in. It was a ferret in a headscarf, a thin quivering nose protruding.

'The wife,' Ellis muttered.

'Any more?' I quipped genially, but they'd both disappeared, leaving a trail of mud along the hall.

I traced them to the dining room, where they stood sizing up the contents. The ferret's nostrils were pinched with disdain. Ellis was about to offer me a two-figure sum for the lot.

I saw at once the folly of my ways. Advertising anything for sale in Gomorrah was tantamount to posting a notice of bankruptcy outside the band club. I'd given myself away.

Getting rid of them was like peeling molasses from an angora sweater. The next morning I was up at seven buying as many copies of the *Gleaner* as I could lay my hands on. I wasn't having my house turned into a tatters' convention. But they still came in droves, so I ended up by selling the telescope to a youth who'd hung about the back door all day shouting 'I wanna be a spaceman.' I thought he at least might get something useful from it. It turned out that he did. He got a second-hand tracker bike from his Uncle Ellis. It was for the part he played in persuading me to part with the telescope at a fraction of the price Ellis intended to get for it once it had mouldered in the ark for a while.

From then on I vowed only to deal with professionals. And no more front-room trading. By now everybody in town knew that the buttons were off the settee. Pocketing my pride, along with various family heirlooms and other trinkets, I went to the jewellers.

'Do you buy gold?' I enquired of the girl assistant, who wore an expression of such absolute boredom it would have persuaded God to revise his Grand Design.

'Only scrap,' she replied, winkling out a lump of mascara from her fingernail with an antique tie-pin.

I withdrew a gold signet ring.

'That's not scrap. That's jewellery.' She didn't deal in jewels, only scrap.

Could she lend me a hammer, I asked, but she ignored the request.

''arold!' she called.

Now you could tell 'arold dealt in jewels, because he had a lazy eye. It was the one that did nothing while the other peered down his magnifying glass. He inspected the ring without enthusiasm before offering me exactly what I paid for it six years ago. I protested. Gold prices had soared.

He shook his head wearily, as though he'd explained it all before to a hundred other shiftless customers like me.

'They've flooded the market, folks like you. Brought the price of scrap right down. That gold's worth next to nowt. When you bought that ring you paid for the workmanship, the retailer's profit, and VAT. No one in their right mind invests in jewellery.'

'You mean, "Lay not treasures up on earth...",' I said.

He nodded and followed the course of his lazy eye, which was straying towards the back room and his beaker of tea.

'Looks like I'll have to go back to being a lily,' I said, half to myself.

I think 'arold would have understood, but the girl laughed out so loud she clouded the silver plate.

I hope she's turned to salt when Judgement Day comes to Gomorrah.

THOSE PINK
REMEMBERED DIVIS

As I sit here reflecting upon ruin, my mind slips gently back. I see a vision of grey terraced houses, slate-tiles shining with rain, dark plumes of smoke curling from every chimney pot. I see cobbled streets running between rows of outside lavatories and brown backyard gates too high to look over. I see a small boy trussed up inside a liberty bodice he hates, because it's cissy, a pair of clogs on his feet that ring on the stone flags between the high-walled backyards, and make smashing sparks when you aim a kick at the pavement. He's clutching a home-made purse held together by a leather thong, and a book that belongs in a drawer in the kitchen and he's not sure what it does but it's called a ration book. And all the way down the street – taking care not to tread on a nick – he's muttering away to himself, so not to forget: 'A quarter o' tea, 'n a loaf o' bread. A quarter o' tea, 'n a loaf o' bread.'

Now before you dismiss all this as the sentimental ramblings of a drowning man, his past life flashing before him as the flood tide of inflation laps about his ears, let me remind you of where this child was going. He was going to the local co-op, a journey made a thousand times by every kid brought up in the back-streets of post-war Northern England. It was a time we once thought of as drab. To me, as new clouds brew, it seems as warm and comfortable as the womb.

Every residential area had its local co-op: a grocer's and a butcher's – cool, still places with mahogany counters and marble slabs and parquet floors when the best we could manage was lino.

The co-op represented permanence, like the Empire must have once been, its windows stacked with pyramids of pineapple chunks and oceans of sarsaparilla on which the sun never seemed to set. And the staff never changed. Spotty apprentices in brown overalls grew whiskers and round shoulders, as they wound away at the giant bacon slicer or tugged at the cheese wire like a giant fret saw. Patient managers checked lists with their indelible pencils until their tongues turned blue as the veins in their faithful wizened necks.

The co-op was as sound and dependable as its blue sugar bags, but sadly, as plain. When the 1950s passed and the brash and flash '60s came swinging in, it began to look as trendy as a faded morning coat. The co-op became a long face in a holiday crowd, as the gloss-paint revolution swept our back-streets and improvement grants fell like confetti from council fingers. It turned its back on us and shut up shop and went to join the East India Company in the history books. And when the canvas-sided pop van failed to return for the empties, when the flour bins were no longer refilled, and the last pale mouse slid disconsolately away, when the winter rain on the tarmacked cobbles sent the last pink divi check floating down the grate, we lost more than a shop. We lost a vital heart to our community.

Now I'm telling you all this, because it accounts for my deep aversion to the modern superstore. Too much cossetting at the knee of the old co-op has handicapped me for the smash and grab of the modern market place. I'm about as at home in a supermarket as a Rochdale pioneer on the board of ICI. But recent circumstances, with which you are by now acquainted, have thrust me cruelly out into the harsh cold world.

People whose souls are pocket calculators and hearts bargain basements have managed to persuade me that penury can be postponed if I start to shop at Superwiz or Money Grub. I have forsaken the convivial queue of the corner shop for a windy trolley park on an industrial estate, and I am about to defy all reason and succumb to the insane logic of the modern super-sell. I'm going to save pounds – by spending them!

My trolley was a crab in its former life, a wilful arthropod with rusty joints. Moving it is like steering a drunk past an open pub door. As I enter the floodlit glare I know just what it's like for a moth to fly inside a lampshade. I become possessed, launching myself dementedly at piles of gleaming merchandise. The pent-up libido that has squirmed through 10,000 mindless television commercials is suddenly released, and I gratify myself in an orgy of purchase. In a flurry of flailing arms I snatch packet after packet of things I would never dream of consuming. I can't wait to get them home and start to

plunge my wicked fingers into their diaphanous outer garments. Oow! It's all too much for my puritan co-operative upbringing, and I collapse next to a deep-freeze into a heap of broken cream crackers and breakfast cereals. A stern old lady with a basket full of catfood pushes her trolley over my foot and mumbles something about winos, and what's wrong with the public library? I cool off by dipping my head into the fridge and pressing my burning cheeks into a pile of steaming chocolate mousses.

Having recovered, I find my trolley's half full. I determine to retrace my steps and put them back. Too late. The alley is blocked by a phalanx of moving trolleys bearing remorselessly down on me. It's like facing the Welsh front-row. I turn and flee towards toiletries.

With a feeling of relief I find myself standing beside a familiar figure.

'How are you, Malcolm?' I ask, settling back into the bath salts to enjoy a good natter. But Malcolm only nods distractedly and reaches out mechanically for a deodorant. A bleeping sound seems to be originating from the region of his armpit. I look closer and see that his wife is at his side, her finger poised upon the buttons of an electronic calculator. She wears the carefree expression of one about to initiate Armageddon.

I point to the aerosol. 'One squeeze and we let another deadly burst of radiation through the ozone belt.' I laugh nervously as I see a manager approaching me suspiciously. 'Who cares, as long as we die smelling sweet?'

The bleep interrupts me and Malcolm's arm drops something else into the basket. He turns and walks woodenly down the aisle leaving me searching for signs of a metal plate and screw holes in the back of his head.

The happy buzz of contented robots is suddenly stilled. A sharp crackle breaks through the narcoleptic music. I hear the words 'Attention! Attention!' followed by a voice that dribbles like glycerine from the hidden loudspeakers.

'It's bargain time again, shoppers, here at Money Grub. Today it's processed peas.'

What about tomorrow? I wonder. But then I'm knocked to the ground. The phalanx has dispersed and formed a ruck round the processed peas.

I try to coax the crab past a shelf of cream cakes only to find that the wheels won't move until I've fed it a box of chocolate eclairs. The trolley is nearly full now. I consult my shopping list to see if there's anything I need amongst all the things I've bought. In the interest of economy I abandon the trolley and go off alone.

When I return the trolley is missing. All the aisles have come to look alike, the products identical. My befuddled brain has retired into the cosy warmth of memory. I remember old Mr Crook at the local co-op who didn't seem to mind whether you paid or not. He used to split five fags for you and accept foreign coins when you'd run out of milk tokens.

Still dreaming, I find a trolley and push it into the check-out queue. I wait while tea-breaks come and go, and keep having to move into another queue. It's like snakes and ladders, without ladders.

My turn comes and everyone behind tuts and stamps as I fumble ineptly, trying to keep up with the tight-lipped automaton that is hurling cartons after me and punching out my requiem on her cash register. It's only when I pick up a packet of budgie grit that I realise I've got the wrong trolley. I didn't want a yellow plastic bath hat, and I don't think I like crispy noodles in cheesy batter. But the automaton has rung up my final total and is waiting like stone for my money.

'What did you want, love?' asked someone, who seemed to have become human again once she'd stepped outside.

'Quarter o' tea, 'n a loaf o' bread,' I whimpered distractedly, clutching my empty purse.

RECIPE FOR DISASTER, OR HE WHO PAYS THE PIE-MAN MUSTN'T CALL THE TUNA

Someone I know went for a job as a reporter on a local newspaper and gasped with dismay when he was told how small his starting salary would be. 'Ah,' said the editor, rummaging through a drawer, 'but it's not so bad. There are certain perks to make things easier for you.' He produced a dog-eared bundle of papers. They were recipes, entitled, 'How to live off nine-and-threepence a week.'

The most celebrated dish was tuna casserole. My friend became renowned for his hospitality. His guest lists for dinner were astonishingly long – this was largely due to cancellations. If the casserole was already in the oven, few got further than the street in which he lived. The neighbours reported him to the local authority, alleging that he'd opened a glue factory in his flat.

I once fought my way through a pack of delirious cats outside his door and got so far as to examine his casserole dish while it was in the oven. The contents resembled a cross between a hedgehog that had strayed on to the M6 and a close-up of the blood-shot eye of a mad bull.

But above all, the tuna casserole was unstable. It was as if the restless spirit of the great fish, trapped for so long in the meagre confines of a can, was suddenly revived by heat. Doubtless mistaking the oven for the warmer waters of its native clime, the contents of the pot would begin to seethe and thresh, and sometimes explode, leaving my friend's kitchen looking like the inside of a Neapolitan tomato purée factory after a terrorist attack.

All copies of the recipe, alas, have now disappeared. In the interest of public safety it was decided to bury them alongside quantities of radioactive waste in an underground silo somewhere in Cumbria.

But the idea isn't dead. It's too good to bury. In fact, I'm thinking of writing to the leaders of British industry to suggest it as a solution to our industrial relations problems. Next time a union submits a pay claim, management could print a few economy recipes. This way we'd have inflation solved in a trice. (Now I come to think of it, I may put myself forward at the next election on this very platform. I could call myself The Tuna Casserole Party!)

But enough of these dreams of vainglory. I myself am now reduced to seeking cheaper ways to eat. And I'm finding as many problems as bones in a neck-end stew.

Take the butcher's. How can anyone who has become known as the Robert Carrier of Khyber Terrace, who flambés his steak puddings, and has campaigned for years to get hollandaise sauce on the counter at the chippie, how can he walk into the butcher's and order half of mince?

There is no surer way of revealing to the world your socio-economic rating than what you buy at the butcher's. Go in and ask for fillet steak and there's such a to-do of forelock tugging you'd think they were plucking a goose. But ask for two slices of corned beef and a cow heel and they throw it at you. And none of these things is cheap any more. Take corned beef. In the war it was held in such universal contempt it might have been made from shot deserters.

Now, if you can find a brand that's not congealed in fat, or brave the rumours of deadly consignments from the Argentine, it'll cost you a king's ransom. The other day I shuffled apologetically down the queue and asked for a pound of ox-tail. 'A pound, sir?' he repeated incredulously. 'People usually buy the whole tail.' I felt like saying that at 60 pence a pound he knew what he could do with the whole tail. He begrudgingly cut it up, making sure I got the thin gristly end that swats flies and made me sick to think about it when I tried to eat it. When I raised the issue of the extortionate price of ox-tail with a retired butcher, who was quietly sipping brandy in the pub, he nodded wisely and said: 'That's because there's only one of 'em. Ha, ha, ha!' Next time I'll try cows' ears. On that principle they should be only half the price.

Helpful and enthusiastic people on the wireless, who probably eat in restaurants, often urge us to try the so-called cheaper cuts. 'Try rolled breast of lamb this weekend,' they say, 'it's simply delicious.' Try it again the next weekend, and you're sure to be dead within the month. That's if you believe half of what the same people say about fat killing. I can't fry a rasher of bacon these days without a vision of choked-up arteries and a heart squirming like a poisoned jelly-fish.

It doesn't seem five minutes ago that everyone was heralding the arrival of the cheap, cholesterol-free and wonderfully adaptable soya bean. Here was something to sate the cravings of the hard-up carnivores. A meat substitute that could be spun into a steak or knitted into a beefburger and was as harmless as a mitten.

Hearing of the stuff, and unable to lay my hands on any by conventional means, I posed as a catering student and paid a call on a local pie-shop.

Now pies are a passion of mine. If fate and desperation hadn't sent me the way of the BBC, I might have been the Leonardo da Vinci of pie-making. My oven has been the mother of the most breathtakingly imaginative and delicious pies. Stand pies that have risen like golden islands in a steamy sea of delicious gravy. Suet pies like ivory palaces crammed with savoury treasures. Patties, exquisite miniatures that make the eye and mouth alike water. I could go on about pies. I have this vision of Utopia: the whole of our turbulent population at peace, while, as one, they sink their teeth into a Smith's pie and let the juice dribble down their chin.

So, you see, it was with a semi-vocational interest that I went to investigate whether there was any truth in the rumour that Rumbelow's were putting textured vegetable protein into their celebrated meat pies. Despite a chef's hat pulled over my eyes and a fair attempt at a baker's handshake, I was treated with the utmost suspicion, once I evinced any interest in the contents of their pies. Old Rumbelow was so jealous of his meat-pie recipe that they say it was never written down for fear of piracy and that he only revealed it to his son on his death bed. But I could see that the son was of a different mould. His pies, he explained proudly, once he knew I wasn't a fifth columnist, were neither pork nor beef. They were cost-accounted. He held up a sickly-looking thing, the colour and texture of a jaundiced corpse. This, for him, was not the symbol of a contented nation, gastric juices in full and happy flood. This was 5p profit. And that – pointing to a tray full waiting for cremation – was two green backs. And the whole thing was selling out in five years' time to a multinational food-chain and settling down in a sun-baked, pastry-free tax paradise.

TVP did, he confessed, play a significant part in his dream. Just how significant he showed me when he took me round the back. There were sacks piled high of TVP, rusk, and other assorted delicacies that formed the staple of his profitable pies. Not a morsel of meat was in sight. It was a miracle. Just what I needed. I purchased a sack of TVP from him at a price that set his face smirking like a crimped pie lid.

I could hardly wait to get home to perform the loaves and fishes trick on my half of mince. As I shook the dry brown pellets of TVP on to the meat, the dog stationed itself at its empty dish and began wagging its tail. Yes, I suppose it did look a bit like dog biscuits. I tossed him a few and watched him circle them suspiciously, before slouching off to sit hopefully outside next door's kitchen.

It looked all right when it was cooked. There was no way you could tell the difference between the processed soya and the meat, except that the mince contained gristle and fat. Only it smelt like cork insoles and tasted like cattle cake – something I may be reduced to trying next, if someone doesn't rediscover the recipe for tuna casserole.

WARDROBE WORRIES

On the eve of my twelfth birthday my mother caught me sniffling unhappily into the sleeve of my green wolf-cub jumper. What was the matter? Had I mislaid my woggle? (or was it a toggle?) Had Akela refused to let me carry the flag in the church parade? What was the matter with the little man? Little man! Boo! That was it. I didn't want to be a little man. I didn't want to get my leaping wolf badge and join the Boy Scouts. I didn't want to wear long pants and get spots. I didn't want to take exams and go to rotten secondary school and make friends with girls. I didn't want to be twelve!

You see, with the visionary powers possessed by all children, I had seen that at twelve you pass through the door that leads out of the green and carefree pastures of childhood and into the concrete quadrangle of adulthood: a place full of rules and responsibilities and dark shadows of miseries like mortgages and matrimonial problems.

Most kids get thrust through this door into adolescence with the sensitivity you expect from a farmer dipping a herd of hoggets. 'Grow up', or, 'Act your age', growl adults, as though it was a simple matter like sloughing off an outer skin and suddenly emerging as a fully fledged consenting tax-payer in a grey suit. You don't get labelled a hooligan or hobbledehoy during that period for nothing. You're a distinctly separate creature, a changeling.

For a long time I put up a spirited resistance to growing up. I wore short trousers, until my knees grew spiky as gooseberries. I played out and got my feet wet, instead of taking ballroom dancing classes. And, as a matter of principle, I read nothing but Enid Blyton's *Famous Five* adventures until I was fourteen. But I had few allies. My chums and erstwhile playmates went rushing into manhood with all the gusto of Johnny Weissmuller taking on a snapping alligator. In the school lavs they handed round soggy-tipped cigarettes like marooned astronauts sharing an oxygen mask. Esoteric literature passed swiftly from one inside pocket to another in the gym queue. And outlandish clothes and hairstyles were sported with the flamboyance of a tribal independence day celebration.

Of course, the authorities took an exceedingly dim view of this. Changelings don't exist, let alone flaunt their identity. There are only children and mini-adults. Lurex suits, dayglo socks, drainpipe trousers and velvet collars were outlawed. So were duffle coats with wooden toggles (or were they woggles?), as well as DAs and Tony Curtis hairdos. (The DA, if you are unfamiliar with the term, was the Tony Curtis worn in reverse – two hanks of hair coaxed into greasy scrolls and hung over your neck so as to resemble the hind-quarters of a common species of water fowl.) We had a headmaster for whom the appearance of a crew cut or a pair of sideboards on one of his boys would bring about a sudden apoplexy. He would jump up and down inside his gown like a flea-ridden jackdaw, ranting about the end of civilisation. Scenes like this had such a marked effect on my tender mind that I truly believed myself to be surrounded by cultural assassins and degenerates. As a consequence, I passed through my early teens submitting to my mother's taste in clothes and the local barber's somewhat restricted repertoire of haircuts – namely, the short-back-and-sides treatment, until my ears stuck out like teapot handles. In a word, I passed for a proper little creep, without an ounce of individuality and destined to crawl from childhood to middle age without stopping anywhere in between. But missed phases, like shirked responsibilities, have a curious knack of cropping up again when you least expect them.

The financial impoverishment that has so cruelly beset my middle years has begun to take its toll on my wardrobe. Solid, once robust worsted jackets now hang limp as failure. Trousers cut to gird a prosperous waist flap disconsolately like windsocks in a breeze. New clothes are desperately needed.

I've never been lucky with sales. Years of sound North Country upbringing – 'You only get what you pay for' – and a certain knowledge that the only knock-down prices are on things nobody wants, have always put me off. But poverty goads me, and there's the obverse side of the Lancashire nature – the love of a bargain, or summat for nowt.

As I stand outside the men's outfitters peering through the slogans: 'Trousers down again!', and 'Contents must be seen to be believed!', a numbing weariness overtakes me. Men's clothes are so unutterably dreary. The same boring colours and conventional styles. I'm not looking for a silver foil boiler suit or doublet and hose, just something striking enough to capture the individuality that's eluded me since childhood.

I step inside and am caught at once. A lizard wearing a tape measure has scuttled out from behind the counter and positioned himself between me and the door. He has a tight, oily skull, a moustache trimmed to a hair's breadth, and is clad in a suit that shines like Esther Williams in a wet swimsuit. He pads towards me in pinched Italian shoes, wringing his hands like a chicken-strangler. He's one of those that isn't going to leave you alone until you've earned him his commission.

'Inside leg'

I feign nonchalance, as though I shared Lord Lichfield's wardrobe. 'Oh, just thought I'd glance at your suits.'

In a flash he's lassooed me round the waist with his tape measure and whipped off my jacket so that the rest of the shop can examine the darns in my woolly. I'm then thrust into a suit nearly as spivvily shiny as his own and told how wonderful I look.

Now I know this type. We used to play a game many years ago. It involved going into an outfitters, grabbing the most awful and unsuitable garment you could find, putting it on and saying: 'Just what I want. How do I look?'

It's doubtless a reflection of the unwillingness of human nature to give offence, rather than the pressures of the commission system of sale, that nine out of ten assistants said just what lizard here was saying. 'Wonderful. You look just wonderful.'

As he began to take down a whole rack of equally unspeakable garments, I thought it was time to employ a survival technique indispensable in moments like this. I pointed towards the window. 'House on fire!' I yelled and grabbing my jacket ran for the door and out into the street for the whole world to inspect my darns.

When sales fail, well-intentioned relatives step in. After all, clan pride is at stake. Word is put about that cousin Phil is down on his luck. His literary agent has eloped with a rural vet. The BBC cuts have struck, lopping off a withered limb. His mum reports that he's looking rather down at heel.

Family wardrobes are searched, dead uncles' suits revived. Parcels smelling strongly of camphor are left discreetly at my doorstep. Trilby hats arrive full of jars of home-made jam. It's as good as a jumble sale, but with none of the public disgrace of being seen there fighting over the oddments.

One spring morning I emerge triumphant from my drab caddis shell of impecunity. A ginger raglan overcoat long enough to sweep the streets, lapels like elephant's ears, a yellow cravat spilling carelessly out. Blancoed spats with just a hint of cracked patent leather peeping through. A green Connemara hat full of fly-hooks. I cut myself a hazel bough and flog a daffodil from next door's garden for a button-hole. Striding casually through the precinct I spy my old headmaster, eighty-three and still looking for truants. I sweep off my hat to him. I can't quite manage a crew cut, but time has graciously bestowed on me a fair imitation of a Yul Brynner. Sir turns purple, jumps up and down and starts shouting for a policeman.

I turn away, happily, complete. Poverty has filled a gap in my life. Who cares if the rest is mothballs.

KEEPING WARM

Some people will tell you that the unadorned human body is a glorious thing. The art schools are full of students screwing up their eyes and brandishing their pencils as they try to capture the fluid sensuality of a goose-pimpled Cindy or the tortured dynamism of Marvin posed as the stricken Prometheus. Others are less enthusiastic. When it's glimpsed on television, they rush to bind the children's eyes and write to the papers of their revulsion and disgust.

I fall into neither of these categories. The sight of the human form divested of its clothes fills me with discomfort. I see only the tragic defect of our species. I can't believe that this smooth-skinned, shivering thing has any part to play in the scheme of things. We're an evolutionary oddity. I know of no other warm-blooded creature like us unless you count whales, and they have acres of fat to compensate. Naked, we are as plucked chickens, newborn hedgehogs, and pigs scraped and scoured and swinging from a butcher's hook. We're pathetic, vulnerable and somewhat ridiculous, all because nature has failed to endow us with any significant quantity of hair.

If you doubt this, why do you think God made all that fuss that morning in the Garden of Eden, when he found Adam and Eve hiding in the bushes trying to cover up their parts like a couple of naughty schoolchildren? You don't suppose *He* was shocked by any of our more curious anatomical features. No. The truth is to be found in the Book of Genesis. There, you'll recall, we're told man was created on the sixth day.

Now, God had had a busy week, all things considered; winding up galaxies and sticking legs on spiders can be pretty tiring. So he probably didn't get round to us until last thing at night. Next morning he came down and it suddenly hit him. 'What have I done! I've forgotten the fur!' But it was too late to do anything about it. It was the Sabbath and that was a rest day, because he'd said so, and it wouldn't do to be the first to break his own commandment. So there we were, in a furry, feathery, scaly, spiny world, as smooth-skinned as a Cox's pippin.

The consequences of this divine blunder have, of course, been catastrophic. Ever since, it's fair to say, by far the most significant part of human activity has been directed at keeping warm. The costly business of keeping a roof over our heads would have been entirely unnecessary had we been blessed with an adequate covering of wool like the common sheep. And fuel bills would cease to be a worry. (Have you never thought it strange that all other animals should shun fire, while we lay waste the planet creating it, burning everything that will burn in a conflagration of smoke and soot that threatens to block out the sun and melt the icecaps?)

It can, of course, be argued that our very vulnerability as a hairless creature has been responsible for our wonderful resourcefulness. Our ancestors didn't spend long grumbling in their draughty caves. They rushed off out and invented the match and the sewing machine. Then, curled up in front of a good fire, snuggling inside the skin of a less resourceful but more hairy creature, they sat back and dreamt up how to split the atom and shower the rest of creation with the blessings of unlimited supplies of heat.

I recall how as a penniless student such resourcefulness came to my rescue. Poverty had confined me to a miserable bed-sitting room whose only concessions to comfort were a single-bar electric heater, a bedside lamp, and a hearth-rug. It wasn't long before I'd learnt to grill bacon over the electric fire, catching the drips on a slice of bread. The hearth-rug doubled as an eiderdown, and the bedside lamp, pushed between the sheets and switched on, did a fair job of airing the bed without setting it on fire more than six times a year.

Now, fat and scant of breath, poverty has again struck, obliging me to return to those student days of youthful enterprise. But luxury has dulled the wits, and things have changed. Modern technology doesn't leave much room for initiative. We lived near the railway then, and you used to be able to pick up a week's supply of good steam coal in an evening's stroll along the line with a sack. Try tapping an overhead wire on Intercity. I had a pal in those days, (I think he's a policeman now) who, because next door used to swank about how well-off they were, drilled through the skirting board and plugged in to their power supply. He was a survivor, revelling in his hairlessness.

The Gas Board having recently joined the electricity people and British Rail as another publicly owned company the majority of the public can no longer afford to use, I decided to rip out the gas fire. The little boy from next door peered up the flue in wonderment. Was it a secret passage? he demanded. I told him that the thing on the roof hadn't always been just for fastening the television aerial to. It was where the secret passage came out, and if he didn't clear off and stop making me feel ancient I'd push him up there with a brush and make him sweep it, like they used to do. He went off to tell his mum that the man next door told lies, leaving me ruefully inspecting a dead starling that had made its grave amongst a pile of soot in the bottom of the grate.

The next thing was to get some wood. I waited until well after dark and visited the bonfire that had been growing on the local rec in readiness for Guy Fawkes night. I reasoned that my needs were greater than an outmoded and dangerous ritual celebrating the antics of some long-dead anarchist. I was just loosening a splendid, tar-impregnated railway sleeper, when about twenty hooligans jumped out of the den in the middle of the bonfire and fell upon me. I tried to explain that I was an inspector from the railways come to reclaim stolen property, but they wouldn't listen and accused me of belonging to a rival gang. I retired to sit in front of an empty grate and count my bruises.

Next day I determined to set out on a logging expedition. Armed to the eyebrows with bow saws and felling axes and towing a battered pram, which I'd hired from the rival gang for 50 pence a day, I combed the local countryside. Piles of dismembered trees that had lain about for years suddenly turned out to be priceless natural resources, the property of jealous and watchful owners. I was wrestling with one sunken log that looked as though it had fallen when the last pterodactyl flew, when some bespectacled ecologist in a camouflaged combat jacket sprang from a bush and began to lecture me on the delicate balance of nature.

Didn't I know that I was removing the vital habitat of a score of fascinating species? If everyone did that, the whole fauna and flora of our island would be under threat. I tried to explain that I was more concerned about the imminent extinction of another creature, much dearer and more fascinating to me than his precious woodlice and toadstools. But it was a waste of time. In any case, I'd probably be dead before the wood caught light, it was so soggy.

Having finally acquired some logs at an extortionate price from a local farmer, that night I sat back to enjoy the old-fashioned luxury of an open fire. Cosily wrapped in my colour supplement fur-fabric bath robe I was sipping my last half a beef stock cube and beginning to feel that God had maybe got it right after all, when there was a knock on the door.

Did I know my chimney was on fire?

I rushed out into the street. Clouds of sulphurous smoke were swirling from the chimney pot, shedding a blizzard of black soot-flakes everywhere. Through the crowd of disapproving neighbours appeared a policeman.

'You do know that this 'appens to be a smokeless zone, sir?'

Everyone must have found this funny, because there was a sudden burst of laughter and they were all staring at me.

'Perhaps we'd better discuss the matter inside, sir,' said the policeman with a diplomatic cough. 'We don't want to add a case of indecent exposure to the charge, do we?'

It was only then that I realised that my bath robe had parted, revealing a significant amount of God's unfinished handiwork.

For the first time for weeks I knew what it was like to feel uncomfortably warm.

KILLER INSTINCT

We once had a spaniel dog who hadn't an ounce of fight in him. He'd been owned by a man who tried to train him as a gun-dog, but found he was a conscientious objector. At the sound of gunshot he fled, and the only time he was ever persuaded to take a bird in the mouth he took it out and gave it a decent burial. He only barked when he was afraid, and his answer to aggression was total submission; he'd roll onto his back with his legs in the air and his eyes tight shut, clearly hoping that the threat would either go away thinking he was dead, or else stay and tickle his tummy.

Just as our dog mysteriously lacked the killer instinct, others possess it, and where you'd least expect to find it. Take the queue at the local greengrocer's, a place you might think would epitomise decency and civilised restraint. After all, the sight of piles of resting Brussels sprouts and wan mushrooms aren't likely to inflame the dangerous passions, not like all that red meat hanging around in the butcher's. Yet, I'm sorry to say, violent scenes are not unknown at our greengrocer's. Little old ladies with forget-me-not blue eyes modestly hidden under copious hats have been known to display all the resolution of a starving fox. And they're just as covert. It was here I was first introduced to the dead leg.

This is achieved by aiming a sharp blow with a heavily weighted shopping basket at the side of the thigh. The result is instant paralysis of the muscles, and the victim staggers sideways out of the queue. Whereupon the little old lady darts forward to order her pound of leeks and ounce of hemlock, before you have a chance to recover. The dead leg leaves no bruising and is hard to distinguish from a sudden attack of cramp. In the circumstances it takes uncommon courage to protest, especially against a concerted hiss of 'Drunk!' from the rest of the queue.

But more subtle tactics are sometimes employed. On one forgettable occasion, when I dared to remonstrate with a woman who, wielding her lead-weighted handbag like a mediaeval mace, elbowed her way to the front of the queue, I was made to feel most wretched. She turned a doleful face towards me, tears conjured from her eyes with all the promptitude of a peeled shallot: 'I've just buried my husband!' she wailed accusingly, as if I'd been his executioner. To a rising chorus of 'Shame!' I fled the queue, blushing like a Worcester pearmain.

Now I have the killer instinct of a Brahmin, so when septuagenarian subterfuge and the 50-pence cauliflower drove me from the greengrocer's queue to growing my own veg, I had all the natural advantages of a one-legged jockey. To this must be added the cultural disadvantage of having come from gardening stock – a long line of horny-handed sons of the sod, who could stun a leatherjacket with a glance, and eat an Eccles cake while stirring a tub of liquid manure. If you think a background like this would have helped, you're wrong. It fostered a lifetime aversion to gardening. From the age of being able to crawl I was sent between the rows of cabbages to weed. To this day I suffer from spinal curvature plus an instinctive reflex action to pluck at anything green and vaguely alien with my first finger and thumb – a habit which on more than one occasion has led to my ejection from English restaurants for interfering with other customers' salads.

Nevertheless, dreams of a stock-scented summer evening, as I sit at my rustic seat listening to the gentle strain of the swelling pea-pods or the potent thrust of burgeoning rhubarb in the galvanised darkness of granny's old dolly-tub have inspired me. It's an irresistible Arcadia.

So I've taken on an allotment. It's not a very romantic word, allotment: a bureaucrat's notion of back-to-nature – half an acre and a rent book and a roll of chicken-wire. Still, however prosaic, it was no preparation for what confronted me one Saturday afternoon, when I arrived with my wellies and spade. Black rotting nettles and a forest of seeded willowherbs 6 feet tall. If I wandered in I might never emerge. Undiscovered tribes might ambush me. Nevertheless, I set to with a will, determined to get the better of nature.

But the moment you break the first sod in a patch of overgrown earth the word seems to spread like wildfire. Dinner. Dinner will be ready soon. Just wait while this mug finishes ricking his back and we can all settle down to a good feed. Birds line the fences, shuffling impatiently, chirruping encouragement. Caterpillars, slugs, wireworms and thrips wriggle, ooze, shimmy and scuttle their way through the surrounding jungle to be there when the first tender seedlings raise their heads. Rabbits drool expectantly. It even gets through to the local cats that you're making a posh new loo up on the allotments. And the kids plot the downfall of your peas and strawberries in summer scrumping missions. Ten thousand hidden eyes are watching you, because the moment you start a garden you're in a state of siege. You are not so much cultivating the land as defending it. And if you haven't the killer instinct, you're as doomed as a carrot in a cannery.

As a child I used to watch my dad with horrid fascination as he wandered amongst the cabbages plucking off the caterpillars and grinding them methodically between his fingers in a splash of green. I've always been a disappointment to him: saving flies from drowning in the bath, giving spiders a leg-up when they fall down the plug hole. I can't even walk down to the local shop on a wet day without rescuing stranded worms from the pavement. The neighbours are convinced I'm reduced to picking up cigarette ends.

So Dad was very proud of me the other day when I asked to borrow his gun. There's been weeks of work clearing and tilling the wilderness, coaxing shoots from seedboxes in the cylinder cupboard, seeing them through intensive care in the cold frame, and then bearing them fondly out into the world like a doting mum. I wasn't going through all this for a buck-toothed little rodent to snip off their heads or a mangy pigeon to tear them out by the roots. I saw things differently now. Mankind hadn't arrived at the pinnacle of creation by rolling on his back and sticking his legs in the air. We'd hacked a bloody trail out of the primal forests, and it was no good letting it all slip through a lot of flabby sentimentality. *The Wind in the Willows* and *Watership Down* were all right for those who got their lettuces in a plastic bag, but for those of us who live off the land, it's nature red in tooth and claw, them or us. I wasn't going to let some snuffling herbivore oust me from the top of the evolutionary tree.

My finger itched on the trigger as I settled down for the night behind the compost heap. A full moon bathed the radish row. My children!

They came like Indians, rabbits in single file, lolloping along, then pausing to sample the air like wine-tasters. There were a lot of small ones. Must have been all one family. Family! That wasn't the way to think of them. They were pests, nasty pests. People never talk about a family of slugs. I waited until they got nearer. The barrel of the gun was a bit bent. Might as well make sure. After all, I could cook them, eat them, make a hat from the skins.

They were settling down to supper amongst the carrots, when I realised one of them had appeared just at the other side of the compost heap. Cheeky beggar! I was just about to squeeze the trigger when he turned to look at me. Moonlight swimming in liquid brown eyes, silver whiskers trembling. How could I? I threw down the gun and stood up. Brothers and sisters scampered off in a flurry of powder-puffs. Brighteyes shrank down into the top-dressing. He'd disappeared, as far as he was concerned, like a child closing his eyes. I bent down and picked him up.

'Look here!' I said sternly. 'I've got to live too. It's either you or me. One of us will have to go!'

The moon-eyes were huge with alarm.

OK. I suppose it might as well be me.

I picked him a carrot.

D-I-Y SPELLS DISASTER

If you believe what you see on commercial television, homes these days are being fitted with an amazing device. Human in appearance only, it runs inexhaustibly about the house, an inanely cheerful grin across its face, terrorising specks of dust and tidemarks, banishing stains, trussing up babies' bottoms in snow-white linen and dishing up quick-frozen dinners; dashing off out to the supermarket to dispense consumer advice to its less enlightened colleagues; luxuriating beguilingly in bubblebaths before dabbing on exclusive toiletries and drifting composedly through fashionable social engagements. The final transformation from a miracle of maternal utility is when, last thing at night, it sinks into something seductive and with a promise gleaming in each eye becomes an alluring plaything.

It is, of course, the ad-man's woman, and I can well understand the irritation of all the persons stuck inside women's skins who have to put up with such insidious stereotyping. But spare a thought for the male person. He's inside a thicker skin, I know, but there's an equally absurd stereotype of him, and I haven't heard quite so many strident voices raised in his defence.

Stereomale, when he isn't faced by the agonising moral dilemma of whether or not to drool over a glamorous female or the froth on a pint of beer, is depicted as the family stooge, bamboozled by convenience catering, having custard pies pushed in his face, and falling off ladders. Or else he's to be seen dancing dementedly around his well-waxed automobile mouthing a jingle, or standing back smugly admiring his resourcefulness as a handyman.

Male conditioning to accept this travesty of individualism is just as remorseless as it is for females. When I was at school, you were pitied as something sexually incomplete if you didn't display an instinctive interest in mechanical engineering. My incurable bafflement at the workings of the internal combustion engine had the authorities thinking seriously about confining me to the needlework class. If I'd been unfortunate enough to have expressed an interest in ballet, I'm sure the boys' changing rooms would have been put out of bounds to me.

Whether or not all women are endowed with the maternal instinct I'm not qualified to say. What I can say, with personal conviction, is that all men are not gifted with the desire or aptitude to become nest-builders. But, it's a role forced upon them by society and, of course, poverty.

It was my next-door neighbour who pointed it out to

me. It had snowed very heavily overnight and everything was carpeted in thick snow. Everything, that is, except my roof. It was as bare as a dunce's slate. 'Loft,' grunted my neighbour knowingly. 'Needs lagging.'

And he was right. For years now, I'd been pumping heat into the sky, megacalories of it. It was probably me who was responsible for the scare about melting the polar icecaps and flooding London. I'd always been puzzled about what was going on up there at sundown. It was like a rookery, flocks of birds squabbling for a square inch to park their claws for the night. And in the morning you could have knocked them off with a stick, they were comatose with the heat.

I made enquiries. The local authority would give a grant. All I needed was for someone to go up there and fill it with straw, or feathers, or whatever it was they did. A little man with bitten fingernails and a wheezy throat came with an estimate. His time would be £5 an hour. £200 a week! I protested. He had his overheads, he argued. I couldn't see what a man who worked in roofs needed with overheads. Wasn't he prepared to take a cut for a starving hack? Think of the service to literature. He thought of it for about half a second, turned on his heel and wheezed his way back to his van and took off.

I resolved to undertake the task myself. First the town hall where I was introduced to the grant form. Was I the landlord or the tenant, demanded the first question. I was neither, I pointed out in some confusion to a fraught secretary. I was the owner-occupier, which surely wasn't the same as being the landlord. A landlord would have tenants, and apart from the starlings on the roof I wasn't aware that I had any. Unless of course there were some to be found in the loft? I had the entire Planning Department debating this semantic nicety before the matter was finally settled by the caretaker who had arrived to empty the ashtrays. By now it was 5 o'clock. 'Tick 'em both,' he advised, with the wisdom of Solomon, 'It'll be reet.'

When six weeks had elapsed I still hadn't heard whether the grant had been approved, and it was getting colder. The form had warned: under no account commence work until approval is given. By now I'd become quite neurotic. Ever since it had been pointed out to me that my heating bills were going up through the roof I'd switched everything off and was living inside an overcoat. 'Ring 'em up,' advised my all-knowing neighbour. When I got through I was told, 'Ay, get stuck in, lad. It'll be reet.' It must have been the caretaker.

The first problem was to get into the loft. I had one, I'd deduced, with much self-satisfaction. Outside, the roof sloped up to a point; inside, the bedroom ceiling was flat. There must be something in between. But there was no trapdoor, and one had to be *made*. I was breaking in to something that had lain undisturbed since the house was built nearly two hundred years ago. I started to quail. Supposing there was a curse. Look what happened to Howard Carter and Lord Carnarvon!

Next door, who'd popped in for a bit of a laugh, advised a polythene sheet fastened to the ceiling to catch the mess. It sounded a good idea. The only trouble was getting my head inside to cut through the laths. It was like being in a Martian duststorm with a leaky spacesuit. Now I knew where wheezy throat got his affliction.

The real reason why I have no aptitude for do-it-yourself activities, is I rush at things. This boy is a spluttermuck! read my school report once. It was for handwork. That teacher had insight. So great is my hatred of such jobs that, never stopping to think, I rush at them to get them over as soon as possible, like jumping into cold water. As a result of spluttermucking, I now had a two-foot square hole in the ceiling right underneath a beam. The obstacle left me with less than 12 inches to crawl through into the roof-space. I toyed with the idea of cutting another trapdoor and labelling them 'entrance' and 'exit', or 'Gents' and 'Ladies'. But the prospect of another hundredweight of soot-clogged plaster was too much. I grunted and squirmed my way through.

Once I'd contrived to get the rolls of wrapping up it was a straightforward enough job. The only problem was to keep your weight on the joists and avoid poking your knees through the laths and plaster of the ceiling below. I was tucking the wrapping under the beam at the far end of the loft when I dropped the torch and it went rolling down inside the eaves and went out. The darkness swallowed me like a coal sack. I started to worm my way under the beam to try and retrieve it when I got stuck. I lay there in the dark unable to move, nose in two hundred years of dust. Suddenly, the thought came scuttling back into my mind like a hungry spider. The curse! What about the curse!

Panic seized me. My shoulders shot out from under the beam like a champagne cork, sending both feet straight through the bedroom ceiling in an avalanche of soot and ancient mortar.

When wheezy throat arrived to replace the bedroom ceiling his rate had risen to £6 an hour. 'What did you say you were?' he asked. 'A writer?'

'I'm the ballet correspondent for *Needlework News*,' I replied bitterly.

He gazed up at the hole in the ceiling. 'I thought as much,' he said. 'Mek us a cup o' tea, luv.'

THE COST OF ENTERTAINMENT

How often have you sat in front of your television set dumb with disbelief at the reactions of a studio audience? Humour that would barely raise a chuckle at a kindergarten teaparty is received with blasts of explosive mirth. Can these be real people? you're moved to ask; real people like you and me?

Any suggestion that it could be canned laughter is usually met with the most vigorous denials by the television companies. Yet I'm quite happy to believe that the art of contrivance has reached such a state of perfection these days that there really is someone in the cutting room whose job it is to take tape from boxes marked 'hefty guffaw' and 'expectant titter', and splice them in where the script is flagging – like a chef popping cloves of garlic and peppercorns into a scrag-end of mutton.

I can think of no other explanation, unless – in the case of the poor BBC – the strained merriment is furnished by staff, threatened with redundancies, and rounded up from the canteen by management, dragged into the studio and told to laugh their hearts out, or else! On the other hand, it could be that the people in the audience are paid to laugh; someone, perhaps, being assigned to wander amongst them with a hat full of £5 notes, dishing them out to those who make most noise. (This is not as unreasonable as it might sound, even in days of economic stringency. What you might save on purchasing a reputable scriptwriter could easily go to softening up the audience, and with a bit to spare.)

When I'm not musing upon this riddle, I'm working out just what it's costing me to be entertained at home. It's £3 a week just to have the television set in the house – that's before you count the cost of the electricity that will bring it to uproarious life and enable me to discern the colour of the custard pies that are flying about. Add to this the cost of trying to keep warm while your mind is being numbed by American crime movies, as well as lighting your way to-and-fro across the room to the off-switch, and I'm beginning to think it's a high price to pay for watching David Attenborough once a week.

It's this kind of consideration that led me to send the set back and search for alternative entertainment. The radio seemed a reasonable choice. It was while I was aimlessly wandering among the margins of the wavebands, in those wastelands of unearthly static, where Babel voices float like lost souls, that I made a most remarkable discovery. Next to the police band – where an anxious constable was heard calling for assistance to eject a party of roisterous television exiles from the nearby Cat and Kettle – I found I could pick up the soundtrack from the television.

Now, a hardy child of hard-up, post-war Britain, I was

no stranger to standing outside the television shop with a flask and sandwiches watching the Cup Final. This discovery called for similar resourcefulness. Discreetly placed outside the front-room window of a neighbour who never draws his curtains, my tranny pressed to my ear, I could have all the advantages of television ownership with none of the cost. I could even turn down the sound without having to move when the maniacal laughter became too much.

I'm convinced that this would prove every bit as edifying as paying good money to stand on the windy terrace of a league football ground for my entertainment. I used to enjoy this until I was one day nigh-on maimed by a missile. Nature having blighted my youth with a premature tonsure that glints like a heliograph in a crowd, my head soon became the obvious target for empty beer bottles discarded by the swaying, chanting mobs behind. Yet I wonder whether I'm fitted for more sophisticated forms of spectator entertainment?

What leaves me in doubt is a recent experience in one of our most celebrated theatrical institutions. I'd scrimped and saved for a ring-side seat at Stratford-on-Avon to watch Hamlet go the full sixteen rounds with his conscience. He's recently come to fascinate me – perhaps I see a mirror of my own melancholy inertia as bankruptcy takes its relentless course. My fatal mistake was to nip into the bar before the performance. Returning to take my seat, I settled down and slid out of my present woes onto the palpitating battlements of Elsinore. The entry of the perturbed spirit coincided with the dreadful realisation that I'd paid for my drink with a £10 note and been given change for only £5! I spent the next two acts totally insensitive to the poetry around me, deep in my own anguished soliloquy, as I debated how I might reclaim what was rightfully mine without murdering the entire bar-staff. As it happened I got my change at the interval, but from the whole unhappy episode I couldn't help but draw the moral that money must take precedence over art in the order of human priorities, and that to open a man's soul to the blessings of poetry, you must first open his purse to the benefits of cash.

The only free entertainment left to enjoy today is conversation. But the conversation-lover is a besieged and lonely figure in this age of sound and fury. The tavern no longer provides the stage for the wit or born story-teller, the traveller with a tale to make the toper lay down his glass. No, he must compete with clattering one-arm bandits and bleeping planetary invaders, billiard cues poked in his ear, or the insidious invisible mush of a light orchestra. I once politely requested that some throbbing jungle sound that was interrupting my closely-reasoned argument for bringing back capital punishment for disc-jockeys, be turned down. I was refused, so I sneaked a hand behind the bar to switch it down myself. I accidentally turned the dial the wrong way. Not a soul batted an ear-flap as the sound swelled by another fifty decibels. They simply screeched that much louder at each other until I was convinced the space invasion had actually taken place and I was surrounded by steel-skulled robots.

Nevertheless, determined to revive the dying art I founded my own Scientific, Literary, and Philosophical Society, opening my doors twice a week to a body of local luminaries that would have made Socrates' gatherings look like a Plastypot party. But it wasn't quite the success I'd hoped for. I was expected to provide copious quantities of refreshment. Nobody, I discovered, talks for talking's sake these days. The most eloquent taproom philosopher grew mute and surly without a glass in his hand. Others seemed to need fuelling like stoves with mountains of cake and sandwiches before I could get a flicker from them. And when it was my turn to dazzle, with all my customary wit and fancy, I'd find their eyes sliding away towards the clock and excuses would be made, and they'd shuffle off to the pub or home to switch on television, abandoning me to the crumbs and empty bottles, and, of course, the bill.

After this I decided to solace myself with a bit of free late-night viewing, courtesy of a neighbour. Clutching my transistor to my ear I crouched in their privet bushes. As I fiddled with the tuning I picked up the local constabulary again, hot on the trail of some peeping Tom. Thinking no more of it I stretched out my feet among the antirrhinums and was settling down to watch Sergeant Bilko, when there was a tap on my shoulder. It was not Eamonn Andrews but a police constable.

At the local lock-up they removed my braces and tie and left me in a cell reciting 'To be, or not to be . . .' By the time morning arrived I'd decided that imprisonment might be my salvation – the one sure way of escaping financial ruin. As long as they gave me a cell-mate who was a good listener. Still, perhaps it didn't matter, one way or the other I was sure of a captive audience. But as my luck would have it I was sent before a lenient magistrate. Instead of putting me away he bound me over and I'd to promise to throw away my radio and get another television at once. I swore to settle down and watch all the comedy shows and laugh in all the right places like a decent law-abiding citizen. I'm still practising and soon hope to be good enough to join a studio audience. I might even get paid for my trouble, for a change. Who knows?